Keith Richards

Printed and bound in Great Britain by MPG Books Ltd, Bodmin

Distributed in the US by Publishers Group West

Published by Sanctuary Publishing Limited, Sanctuary House, 45–53 Sinclair Road,
London W14 0NS, United Kingdom

www.sanctuarypublishing.com

ISBN: 1-86074-590-3

Keith Richards

Alan Clayson

Sanctuary

To Pete Cox

'Keith Richards is a normal guy living, by all accounts, in the body of Superman. By all the rules of the game, he should no longer be here.'

Frank Allen of The Searchers

Contents

About The Author

Born in Dover, England in 1951, Alan Clayson lives near Henley-on-Thames with his wife Inese. Their sons, Jack and Harry, are both at university.

A portrayal of Alan Clayson by the *Western Morning News* as the 'AJP Taylor of the pop world' is supported by *Q*'s 'his knowledge of the period is unparalleled and he's always unerringly accurate.' He has penned many books on music – including the best-sellers *Backbeat*, subject of a major film, *The Yardbirds* and *The Beatles Box* – and has written for journals as diverse as *The Guardian, Record Collector, Mojo, The Times, Ink, Mediaeval World, Folk Roots, Guitar, Hello!, The Independent, Ugly Things, The Times* and, as a teenager, the notorious *Schoolkids Oz*. He has also been engaged to perform and lecture on both sides of the Atlantic – as well as broadcast on national TV and radio .

From 1975 to 1985, he led the legendary Clayson And The Argonauts, and was thrust to 'a premier position on rock's Lunatic Fringe' (*Melody Maker*). As shown by the existence of a US fan club – dating from a 1992 *soirée* in Chicago – Alan Clayson's following grows still, as well as demand for his talents as a record producer, and the number of versions of his compositions by such diverse acts as Dave Berry – for whom he played keyboards in the mid-1980s – and New Age outfit, Stairway. He has worked, too, with The Portsmouth Sinfonia, Wreckless Eric, Twinkle, The Yardbirds, The Pretty Things and the late Screaming Lord Sutch, among others. While his stage act defies succinct description, he has been labelled a 'chansonnier' in recent years for performances and record releases that may stand collectively as Alan Clayson's artistic apotheosis, were it not for a promise of surprises yet to come.

Further information is obtainable from www.alanclayson.com.

Prologue
Mr Showbusiness

'I almost prefer the 1961 style of interviews: favourite colours or "Helen bounced into the room". Wasn't it amazing then? A Star could do no wrong.'

– Keith Richards[1]

You probably know the bare bones of the story already. Keith Richards' career left the runway in 1963 when The Rolling Stones' maiden single, a version of 'Come On' by his eternal hero, Chuck Berry, hovered on the edge of the Top 20. He was co-writer of most of their subsequent smashes, snatching control of the group's destiny from the fated Brian Jones – the Snowball to Keith's Napoleon as Mick Jagger was the Morecambe to his Wise.

Chewed upon and spat out by the Swinging Sixties, Richards then fought a hard-won battle against heroin addiction, but was still responsible for the lion's share of songs on 1972's *Exile On Main Street* double album, which today's pop pickers have been brought up to regard as the Stones' finest collection. Nearly all consequent offerings featured at least one lead vocal by Keith, who otherwise ministered to overall effect with a guitar style that earned him the *sobriquet* 'The Human Riff'.

Today, the wild youth who recorded 'Come On' has entered a graceful old age as a distinguished, charitable and humorous musician who, almost despite himself, has become a British showbusiness treasure – and when you've reached that plateau, another hit record is a mere sideshow.

The first autobiography dedicated to Keith alone appeared in 1982, and there have been several more since, most of them tending to deal too hastily with his two decades before 'Come On', years that were at least as intriguing as those of any more exalted and chronicled eras. With this in mind, I screwed myself up to talk to complete strangers about matters that took place up to half a century ago – as well as wading through oceans of archive material.

Some of my findings shattered minor myths, and some of his ruminations in print – albeit convivial burblings that he may have believed were off-the-record to others who weren't in the mood for sensible dialogue either – bore out Frank Zappa's much quoted, 'Rock journalism is people who can't write interviewing people who can't talk for people who can't read.'[2]

Richards got on my nerves slightly too with conversational tics, instanced most conspicuously by his constant reference to young women as 'chicks'. He probably doesn't realise he's doing it any more. There were also a few contradictions. For example, were the tenants who lived on the ground floor of the grim Chelsea flat he shared in 1962 with Mick and Brian, 'chick [*sic*] teachers from Sheffield and Nottingham', as he insisted in 1988[3], or 'four old whores from Liverpool –real old boots they were' as he described them 17 years earlier?[4]

Yet, as Horace reminds us, '*quandoque bonus domitat Homerus*' – which, given a free translation, means even the wisest can make mistakes. If Keith Richards is guilty of factual error, it's only to be expected from one whose 60-odd years on this planet have been neither quiet nor unblurred by experiences that might have warped or created holes in his memory.

I am, therefore, grateful for help received from several sources that prefer not to be mentioned – as well as Pat Andrews, Dave Berry, Don Craine, Keith Grant-Evans, Phil May, Jim McCarty, Dick Taylor and Art Wood for their reminiscences, clear insight and intelligent argument.

Please put your hands together too for Iain MacGregor, Chris Harvey, Diana Bell, Tara O'Leary, Dicken Goodwin, Albert Depetrillo, Michael Wilson, Kathleen Meengs, Claire Musters and the rest of the team at Sanctuary.

Whether they were aware of providing assistance or not, let's have a round of applause too for these musicians: Frank Allen, Roger Barnes, Alan Barwise, Peter Barton, Mike Cooper, Pete Cox, the late Lonnie Donegan, Chris Gore, 'Wreckless' Eric Goulden, Brian Hinton, Robb Johnston, Garry Jones, Graham Larkbey, Tom McGuiness, Brian Poole, Tom Robinson, Jim Simpson, Mike and Anja Stax, the late Lord David Sutch, John Townsend and Paul Tucker.

Thanks is also due in varying degrees to Stuart and Kathryn Booth, Robert Cross (of Bemish Business Machines), Kevin Delaney, Peter Doggett, Ian Drummond, Katy Foster-Moore, Richard Hattrell, Michael Heatley, Dave Humphries, Rob Johnstone, Allan Jones, Mick and Sarah Jones, Elisabeth McCrae, Russell Newmark, Mike Ober, Mike Robinson, Mark and Stuart Stokes, Anna Taylor, Michael Towers, Warren Walters, Gina Way and Ted Woodings as well as Inese, Jack and Harry Clayson.

Alan Clayson
May 2004

1 The Kentish Man

'An only child loses much that makes for happiness and for character formation, and if a couple can afford one child, they can afford two.'

– Rose Hacker[1]

Whether through financial restrictions, inability to conceive a sibling for him or the gradual estrangement that lead eventually to his parents' marital breakdown, Keith Richards came to embody many common characteristics of the only child. Though self-contained and adept at entertaining himself, all he had to do was cry to gain undivided attention and be reassured by mother Doris, if not father Bert, of how adorable and special he was, at least in the cosy world of Chastillian Road. This was the family home where he was brought after his birth on 18 December 1943 in the local Livingstone Hospital in Dartford, the market and industrial town just beyond East London's creeping smog and mile upon mile of Albert Squares.

As Dartford was west of the Medway, Keith was a 'Kentish Man' as opposed to a 'Man of Kent'. Certainly, he was as far from the White Cliffs of Dover's mythical bluebirds as it was feasible to be without leaving the county referred to as the 'Garden of England' by straight-backed old maids free-wheeling on sit-up-and-beg bicycles with basketwork carriers down rolling country lanes to Evensong in the mellow sunshine of parting day.

The Richardses neither freighted household vocabulary with PG Woodhouse-esque phrases like 'jolly good' and 'right-ho!' or dwelt in an olde-worlde arcadia of meadows and woodland. Nevertheless, sooty foxgloves might have sprung up beneath sepia skies on the bomb sites that remained after the Luftwaffe's pounding of the docks along the waterfronts of the quickly over-populated conurbation of the 'Medway Towns' that fanned out from Chatham and Gillingham.

From Dover to Glasgow, sirens and alarm bells executed discordant threnodies around buildings either crumbling in a haze of smoke and powdered plaster or being blown more cleanly out of existence by direct hits throughout nightly aerial bombardments. 'If you were a "war baby", it was a bit gloomy and grey, and everything was bomb-struck,' remembered Keith, 'It was nothing to turn a corner and see nothing on the horizon apart from one or two miracle houses. You grew up in a wasteland.'[2]

On emerging from babyhood, Keith's hair had remained black. His ears were jug-handle, his features angular, his build slim and his respiratory system troubled by hay fever.

Some French blood was inherited from Doris, whose maiden name was Dupree. Her and Bert's eyes had first locked in the metropolitan clerking office where they both worked. After a three-year courtship they married in 1936. By then, Bert's new job in a light-bulb factory involved a long daily commute to Hammersmith on the furthest side of London, and a longer spell on the assembly line where he rose to the rank of foreman.

Then the War Office, nervous about the stalemate its forces had reached against the Axis powers, sent for Bert Richards. While serving in the Bedfordshire and Hertfordshire Regiment, he was wounded in the leg in 1944, and spent the rest of the war in an orthopaedic hospital in Mansfield. Demobilised, he slipped back into the old routine at the factory with astonishing swiftness. A wearied gazer from the window of a passing train, Mr Richards got up, got to work, got home and got to bed, spending little 'quality time' with an ideally seen-but-not-heard son.

Rendered taciturn by an exhaustion that seemed to hover perpetually over him, Bert betrayed little overt emotion towards Keith beyond irritation – particularly if disturbed during the armchaired, pipe-smoking hours in front of the television, around which his evenings revolved from the mid-1950s. This – and Bert's stolid compliance to ingrained 'decent' values – was balanced by his more free-spirited wife, who supported the boy's activities with a zeal that her many sisters might have thought excessive. Though he was the sole focus of Doris's hopes and expectations, she didn't impose any ambition by proxy upon Keith – imagining him, say, as a solicitor, a doctor or even another Bert. Indeed, in the relaxed and informal atmosphere that pervaded while his father was out of the house, Keith was given free rein to do things on his terms, in his way and whenever he was in the mood.

He wasn't, therefore, as prepared as he might have been for confronting the competitive world of Westhill Infants School where a grizzling, garbardine-raincoated child was delivered, cradled in his mother's arms, on the first morning. Acquiring a reputation as a bit of a cry-baby in the playground, he was also rather a shrinking violet when obliged to approach the teacher's ink-welled desk with an exercise book. There were indications of a flair for art and creative writing, although he was loathe to take literary risks for fear of being told off, bemused as he was by the unimaginative regime epitomised by multiplication tables chanted *en masse* to the rap of a bamboo cane, and cross-legged music lessons around the upright piano in a main hall that also served as gymnasium, dining room and venue for the prayer-hymn-prayer sandwiches with which Church of England schools usually began the day.

More exciting than 'We Plough The Fields And Scatter' and the BBC Home Service schools broadcasts' John Barleycorniness were the sounds that effused from the Light Programme, the station from which the radio dial rarely moved when Doris was engaged in household chores. Its programming, however, was not entirely counter to school dictates of what was 'good' music. Though you'd be brought up short by, maybe, Billy Cotton and his Band blasting up 'Waltz Intermezzo' from Mascagni's *Cavalleria Rusticana*, more typical were muzak arrangements of Handel, Offenbach and Rossini oozing from the orchestras of Mantovani or Geraldo, as well as light opera arias from the likes of Mario Lanza and Josef Locke.

The Pavarotti of his day, Lanza was to come within an ace of Number One in the newly established *New Musical Express* – (*NME*) record sales chart in 1952 when, after transfer to Wentworth Primary School – the consequence of the Richards family moving to Morland Avenue in an adjacent suburb – it was discovered that Keith required little coaxing to participate, even sing solo, in class assemblies. Battle hardened now, he was also putting up his fists, looking fierce and hoping for the best in the uglier playtime disputes that were generally concluded in the Head's study with the swish of cane on buttocks or outstretched palm.

Of the teachers who warmed to the new pupil was a Mr Clair. In charge of the choir, he included Keith in an ensemble destined to appear in the finals of an inter-school competition at no less than the Royal Albert Hall. That a future Rolling Stone was also among the massed choristers, so the story goes, at the Queen's televised coronation in Westminster Abbey on 2 June 1953 was not appreciated at the time either – although Keith himself was to acknowledge that 'Jake Clair taught me a lot', albeit with the reservation, 'After my soprano went at thirteen, singing was over for me. I only got into singing again after finding out that I could write songs.'[3]

Keith's musical talents came from his mother's side of the family. Her father, Theodore Augustus Dupree, was a multi-instrumentalist versatile enough to have blown saxophone when dapper in immaculately stiff evening dress on a palais bandstand in the 1930s, and to have bowed weepy fiddle in a check-shirted post-war country-and-western outfit. Rather than the light 'sweetcorn' of Slim Whitman and Jim Reeves, the latter group favoured the 'hard' approach of Hank Williams and his Drifting Cowboys with their unusual absorption with rhythm. This hinged on singing composer Williams' own guitar chopping and a repertoire that owed almost as much to the blues as it did to country and western.

As Williams' fame spread beyond the USA's Deep South, his records were covered for the pop market by the likes of Tony Bennett and Rosemary Clooney – and evidence suggests that, but for his drug-induced death in 1953 at the age of 29, he might have shared the mainstream popularity of this syrupy elite – and that of the upstarts that superseded them. 'You should never underestimate the importance of country in rock 'n' roll.' Keith would pontificate later.[4] Yet, though he was talking about the music, Richards was also aware that Hank Williams was a prototype too for rock 'n' roll's anti-hero. Likewise, US *film noir* actors James Dean – the 'Rebel-Without-A-Cause' – and Marlon Brando, leather-clad leader of a motorbike gang who mumbled his way through 1954's much-banned *The Wild One*, were also role models that caused Keith and other sham-tough lads half a world away in northeast Kent (even those who hadn't actually seen Brando or Dean on screen), to saunter down to corner shops with hunched shoulders, hands rammed in pockets and chewing gum in a half sneer.

The United States of America seemed the very wellspring of everything glamorous – from Coca-Cola to The Ink Spots, whose humming polyphony had enraptured the kingdom's theatres during a 1947 tour. Concern was to be expressed ten years later in a feature in *Everybody's Weekly*, a now defunct something-for-everybody journal. 'Are We Turning Our Children Into Little Americans?'[5], it asked – for, as well as crew cuts bristling on young scalps and Barkis remarking that Mrs Peggotty 'sure knows her cooking' in a US cartoon-strip edition of *David Copperfield*, almost as incredible were the Wild West films that British youth had come to consume. No one ever talked thataway. Neither would a pub landlady fail to bat an eyelid if some hombre was plugged full of daylight in the lounge bar. A god had descended on London once when Roy Rogers rode *a Trigger* from his hotel to Leicester Square Odeon cinema. To many youngsters – including Keith Richards – Rogers, Gene Autry, Hopalong Cassidy and other singing cowboys with guitars, albeit more 'sweetcorn' than 'hard', were significant early influences.

On the cusp of adolescence, Keith was dazzled too by presentations that marked the passing of the English music hall. He could forget about spelling tests and times-tables as a magician sawed his buxom assistant in half, and Max Miller told the one about his wife and the nudist who came to use the telephone. It was called 'music hall' because each artiste made use of the pit orchestra, if only for a rumble of timpani as a rabbit was produced from a top hat.

Usually, the bill would contain an entirely musical act; a singer more often than not. As the 1950s got out of neutral, however, you'd be less likely to be serenaded with 'Danny Boy', 'The Loveliest Night Of The Year' or like warblings from the repertoires of Locke and Lanzo than 'How Much Is That Doggie In The Window?' or 'Mambo Italiano' from less round-vowelled vocalists in the *NME* Top Ten. Yet, for want of anyone better, Ronnie Hilton, a former apprentice engineer from Leeds with a neo-operatic tenor, was cited in the *NME* as 1955's most popular British vocalist. His rival as the BBC's most omnipresent singer was Lee Lawrence, a former serviceman with a similar style.

Aware of pop music from infancy, Keith Richards' search for teenage music on the Light Programme had resulted in no allegiance to any specific star, though he preferred Nat 'King' Cole's less mannered version of 'Because You're Mine' to that of Mario Lanza, and specific items, such as Hoagy Carmichael's 'Hong Kong Blues' and Billy Eckstine's 'No One But You', twisted his heartstrings occasionally. He recognised too that Carmichael's technique was 'very country, very laconic and dry. I like the ambiguity he gets. I want words to pull triggers.'[3]

With either Hoagy on the wireless or Brando before him on the front cover of *Picturegoer*, Keith might have said with Wordsworth that 'to be young was very heaven' when fooling himself that he was having a good time in the screaming drabness of post-*bellum* Dartford, despite another – and rather disagreeable – uprooting from Morland Avenue to Spielman Road in Temple Hill, a council estate of raw red brick.

On the opposite pavement, a couple of neighbourhood ne'er-do-wells glared with gormless menace as the newcomers unloaded their furniture. Out for more than boyish mischief, they returned to the streets after dark as part of an aimlessly swaggering phalanx that other pedestrians would cross roads to avoid. In 1954 on a London heath, a meek if vulgar reproof, 'you flash cunt', by the victim had precipitated the first Teddy Boy murder. After that, there had been questions in Parliament, hellfire sermons and films, such as *Violent Playground* and *Cosh Boy*, that suggested that flogging was the only way to tame these hybrid Mississippi cardsharps and Edwardian rakes who wrecked church youth clubs, snarling with laughter as a with-it vicar in a cardigan pleaded ineffectually. With brilliantined and effeminate cockades offset with scimitar-like sideburns, and brass rings decorating their fingers like knuckledusters, they'd barge *en bloc* into dancehalls without paying. If you so much as glanced at them, the next piece of action could be *you*.

The Teds could be secretively anti-social too, slitting cinema seats with penknives during showings of *Blackboard Jungle*. Keith had caught this melodrama, which was set in a run-down

New York high school, when it arrived in Dartford, but had been as riveted by the music behind the introductory credits as the plot. Like all but the most serious-minded children of the 1950s, he had been thrilled, superficially anyway, by 'Rock Around The Clock' by Bill Haley And The Comets.

More pivotal than any frame of *Blackboard Jungle*, nonetheless, was an illicit tuning in to Radio Luxembourg when suffocating under bedclothes as the small hours were illuminated by the dial of one of these newfangled pocket transistors. Under such conditions, Keith Richards first heard Elvis Presley and Little Richard: 'They played "Heartbreak Hotel" and "Long Tall Sally" – and the ad for the Irish sweepstakes followed. I was supposed to be asleep. It was an electrifying night for me. I knew from the minute I heard Elvis that that's what I wanted to do.'[6]

A more profound impression was created by the heart-stopping second guitar break in Presley's 'Hound Dog', and, predating that chronologically but issued in Britain later, a solo by the same musician, Scotty Moore, in 'I'm Left You're Right She's Gone'. 'I could never work out how he played it,' marvelled Keith, 'and I still can't. It's such a wonderful thing, I almost don't want to know.'[4]

Once, the instrument had been associated mainly with Latinate heel-clattering, but now it was what Elvis – and, if you read the small print, Scotty Moore – played. At grandfather Dupree's house in Primrose Hill, North London, a guitar lay on top of the piano in the sitting room. Sometimes he let the untutored Keith mess about with it, investigating sounds rather than notes.

Back in Dartford, in a time-honoured ritual of thwarted eroticism, the boy would shape up in front of a wardrobe mirror, his hands gripping an imaginary guitar. He'd pretend to slash chords and pick solos with negligent ease, perhaps feigning a collapse and crawling to the edge of a stage to the delight of thousands of ecstatic females that only he could see, 'I got the moves off first, and I got the guitar later.'[7]

Keith had had nothing saved up, but Doris conjured up, from her wages as a part-time shop assistant, the down-payment for an acoustic guitar of indeterminate make – possibly a Rosetti – on hire-purchase. Boosted too by her jocund encouragement and some pointers from his grandad, Keith positioned yet-uncalloused digits on the taut strings and laboured late into the evening, to the detriment of even that modicum of homework necessary to avert the big stick or a detention the next day.

Not especially assiduous in tracking his son's academic progress either, Bert objected only when Keith's tinkerings – in a favoured place at the top of the stairs or in the bathroom (for echo) – discomposed his quietude in front of the television. After all, he had to be at the factory, fresh and alert, while some he could mention were yet to stir.

Keith's fingertips hardened with daily practice, and it occurred to him – and Doris, egging him on over the ironing – that he had an intangible something else that was missing in the guitarists on the discs he was trying to emulate. He may have supposed that it was because they span on the cheap record player Doris had bought at the Co-Op, but apparently it was the same on the most expensive and cumbersome mahogany radiogram. Was it the records themselves? Much of 15-year-old Keith's collection consisted of releases on Embassy, a domestic budget label that contracted artists whose very lack of individuality was ideal for cranking out xeroxes of other people's hits.

Sometimes up to half-a-dozen tracks were squeezed onto an EP (extended play) pressing. 'Can you tell the difference between these and the original sounds?' was Embassy's rhetorical question on one such tacky sleeve. Indeed you could, but only the occasional misjudged timbre of too-plummy lead vocals or a butter-fingered instrumental phrase made such merchandise 'so-bad-it's-good'.

An Embassy entity called The Canadians with Ken Jones And His Band virtually re-wrote 'Blue Suede Shoes', but the general aim was to be proficient copyists of whatever pop commotions were stirring up the nation. Yet even when an Embassy session player copied Scotty Moore note for note, it was somehow too bland and inhibited with no 'feel' for rock 'n' roll. When this great light dawned, Keith decided that it was a false economy to save nearly two shillings for an ersatz 'That'll Be The Day' by a Briton called Hal Burton that bore as much relation to the template by The Crickets as low-fat margarine did to dairy butter. Therefore, he shelled out the full six shillings and eight pence for Buddy Holly's resonant guitar break gnawing at the song rather than Billy Cotton-esque brass.

Holly, The Crickets' X-factor, had come into his own when the hunt was up for more moneymakers in the Presley mould. Needless to say these sprouted thickest in North America, where some heard Jerry Lee Lewis as just an Elvis who substituted piano for guitar. Possibly for that reason, Keith hadn't been keen on Lewis in the first instance. Yet, as self-obsessed as a genius can be, the self-styled 'Killer' thrived on an electrifying stage presence that displayed plurality of taste, unpredictability and a forgiven arrogance in compatible amounts. Serenity wasn't Jerry Lee's way offstage either, riven as his years were with high living, destitution, stimulant abuse, arrests, more marriages than Henry VIII, last-minute tour cancellations, his shooting of a bass guitarist and the accidental deaths of two sons and a wife. There were also the bouts of loud piety that recurred from a poor upbringing within the clang of the Assembly Of God Church bell in Ferriday, Louisiana.

All manner of further variations on the Presley blueprint were arriving by the month. After Carl Perkins, an unsexy one, there had been bespectacled Holly and unsexy *and* bespectacled Roy Orbison, with his eldritch cry and misgivings about the up-tempo rockers he was made to record by Sam Phillips, owner of

Sun – the Memphis studio where Elvis – and Jerry Lee – had first smouldered onto tape. There were female Presleys like Wanda Jackson and Janis Martin; mute ones in guitarists Duane Eddy and Link Wray; a crippled one in Gene Vincent ('The Screaming End'); two-for-the-price-of-one in The Everly Brothers and a clean-cut latecomer in Ricky Nelson. In parenthesis, the latter's 'Poor Little Fool', as duplicated by an Embassy hireling, had been, purportedly, the first record Keith Richards ever owned.

Crucially, there were black Elvi too.[8] Among the most ear-catching for Keith would be shrieking Little Richard beating hell out of a concert grand in *The Girl Can't Help It*, which reached the Medway Towns in 1957. Nonetheless, it was 'Lucille', the follow-up to the hit single of this movie's title theme, that convinced Richards that rock 'n' roll was going to last far longer than hula-hoops, the cha-cha-cha and previous short-lived fads: '"Lucille" is the one that first turned me on, that made me think rock 'n' roll's here.'[4]

However, of all the Grand Old Men of classic rock, the first and foremost for Keith was, and would always be, Chuck Berry, whose first entry in the US *Hot 100*, 'Maybelline', had actually predated 'Heartbreak Hotel'. Like Hank Williams – and Presley's first essays as a recording artiste – it had as much to do with country and western as it did blues.

As his name will surface as regularly as rocks in the stream in this account, it may be useful to outline Berry's background in some detail. He was born Charles Edward Berry in 1926 – or 1931, according to early press releases – and raised in St Louis, Missouri. With the onset of puberty, he became a singing guitarist and began composing when leading his own trio. His output was flavoured with the most disparate ingredients in the musical melting pot of the Americas: Cajun, calypso, vaudeville, Latin, country and western, showbiz evergreens and every shade of jazz – particularly when it was transported to the borders of pop via, say, the humour of Louis Armstrong, the rural stumblings of the Mississippi delta, and Chicago and New Orleans rhythm and blues.

Berry turned professional at the age of 26 in a group named after its pianist, Johnnie Johnson. When rechristened The Chuck Berry Combo, the outfit worked local venues with occasional side trips further afield to the Cosmopolitan Club in Chicago – where blues grandee Muddy Waters was so sincerely loud in his praise that Berry was signed to the Windy City's legendary Chess label in 1955.

After 'Maybelline' peaked at Number Five in the *Hot 100*, 'Roll Over Beethoven' climbed almost as high. Next, 1957's 'School Days (Ring! Ring! Goes The Bell)' came close to topping the list. With melodies and R&B chord patterns serving as support structures for often erudite lyrics celebrating the pleasures available to US teenage consumers, another rich commercial year generated further smashes in 'Rock And Roll Music', 'Sweet Little Sixteen' and Chuck's 'Johnny B Goode' signature tune.

Transfixed, Richards started buying Berry discs without first listening to them in one of the isolation booths that record stores had in those days – and it was a magazine picture of Chuck on the wall that greeted him when he first yawned and stretched in the grey of morning. 'England was black and white,' he would reminisce, 'and, suddenly, everything went technicolor,'[4] with Berry in the most vivid hues of all, despite no major penetrations in the British charts. He had been first experienced by the world beyond the States when he appeared in *Jazz On A Summer's Day*, a US film documentary about a turn-of-the-decade outdoor festival. Derisively 'duck-walking' with his crotch-level red guitar, Chuck offended jazz purists but captured the imaginations of European teenagers who were to turn to his Chess LPs as frequently as monks to the Bible.

Emulation of heroes is a vital part of growing up, and the essence of Keith's fretboard style was formed with Berry lurking in the background. 'When I started,' he confessed, 'I pinched virtually all his riffs.'[9]

From absorbing Berry and, to a lesser degree, other US icons like blotting paper, Richards dug deeper: 'Jerry Lee Lewis and Chuck Berry were a lightning bolt to kids of my generation, and they led you to other things. Chuck was at Chess, and so was Muddy Waters, so you go through the roster of Chess, Sun, Red Bird... Then I looked at the names of the musicians on Chuck Berry records, and the ones for Bo Diddley, Muddy Waters...same cats. So you want to be one.'[6]

In Britain in the late 1950s, you couldn't so much as approach the foothills of such a vocational Olympus. The only openings for one such as Keith was via skiffle, a craze that, if born of the rent parties, speakeasies and Dust Bowl jug bands of the US Depression, had sprung up during a rummaging for a native riposte to Elvis. The job had gone to Tommy Steele, a young merchant seaman, but his 'Rock With The Cavemen' had been shut down in 1956's autumn Top 20 by 'Dead Or Alive' from Lonnie Donegan, regarded as 'The King of Skiffle' during his prime. His first chart climber, 'Rock Island Line', also harried a US Top 40 upon which UK records had seldom encroached.

Another such disc to make it there – but only just – was 'Freight Train' by The Chas McDevitt Skiffle Group with Nancy Whiskey, a Glaswegian lass, on lead vocals. It too took coals to Newcastle in that it was an upbeat arrangement that belied the gloomy lyrical content of the 1905 composition by black gospel singer Elizabeth Cotton.

Three months after its release, a place was found for a performance of 'Freight Train' in the bio-pic *The Tommy Steele Story*, and it earned the approbation of the blossoming nuclear disarmament movement when re-worded as 'H-Bomb' by John Brunner. Nevertheless, its unexpected success in the States made it necessary for Whiskey and McDevitt to risk losing momentum at home in order to appear on *The Ed Sullivan Show* and other prestigious television slots – as well as a handful of stage shows – with hastily rehearsed US musicians.

That, as far as the North American public was concerned, was that for Whiskey and McDevitt, and any further examples of British skiffle – apart from 'Does Your Chewing Gum Lose Its Flavour', a 1961 postscript from Donegan. Nevertheless, skiffle was as contagious as bubonic plague at home – with every vicinity cradling such entertainers enjoying parochial fame. From where London bleeds into Kent, a Peter Smith, strumming a home-made guitar, made a public debut with The Hard Travellers at a staff party in a hospital in Swanley, the most far-flung Medway Town. The group leaned towards country and western, though the repertoire also embraced the expected classic rock and Top 20 preferences as well as one or two of Peter's first offerings as a composer.

After assuming the *nom de théâtre* 'Crispian St Peters', Smith was to flower momentarily as a 1960s pop star – as would a skiffler from Croydon, Ralph May, in the 1970s, having adopted the stage surname 'McTell' in genuflection to a Mississippi bluesman, before taking to the road like dust bowl balladeer Woody Guthrie, 'armed only with a guitar and a pocketful of dreams'.[10]

McTell was, however, just finding his feet at grammar school in 1956's autumn term, while the slightly older Keith Richards was at Dartford Technical School, an educational option that was more likely to lead to a trade apprenticeship than university. Though he'd lasted a few weeks as a boy scout, Keith had long nurtured a resentment of any form of hearty clubbism inherent in this and similar after-school activities, and a distrust of adult authority figures. This impacted on his sojourn at the Technical School where there was constant turmoil over his speech, his manners, his slouch, the 'crude' drainpipe jeans he wore every day to go with the purple shirt, winkle-pickers and denim jacket – and him sculpting his hair in that ridiculous quiff-and-ducktail style, like one of those Teddy Boys that still prowled the evening streets in packs, looking for things to destroy and people to beat up.

Comparing notes in the staff room, teachers agreed that that Richards lout had an 'attitude' as bad as the pimples that erupted constantly on his face. Much of it stemmed from extra-curricular pursuits that had little bearing on what he was meant to be studying. Not standing when he could lean, he was a known truant with the *leitmotif* of petty shop-lifting and seeking refuge in amusement arcades and snooker halls or having his nose glued against motorbike showroom windows. More long term was the smoking that he'd never have the will to stop.

In class, Richards tended to lounge in the back row, dumbly insolent and indifferent to ox-bow lakes and Euclid's knottier theorems. Relieved when he was absent, both wrinkled senior master and trainee on teaching practice found it less stressful to apply a brake to the sarcastic *bon mots* and, as far as they were able, ignore him altogether.

With almost mathematical precision, Keith's slothful and disorderly behaviour had him slacking among pupils a year his junior and then expelled from Dartford Technical School without any formal qualifications at 16, which was the minimum school-leaving age at the time. He was advised that the Youth Employment Centre might not find him beyond redemption. Alternatively, he could do worse than join the Regular Army. At the opposite end of the spectrum, however, was enrolling at an art college in nearby Sidcup, more London than Kent. Entry standards were lax to the point of being non-existent beyond evidence of a slight artistic turn – though Phil May, who began at Sidcup in September 1960, qualified this with, 'The only way you could get into that art college without GCE 'O' levels was by doing graphic design. I got in when I was 15 after they'd seen my Bexleyheath secondary modern school portfolio. David Hockney told me that if there'd been General Certificates of Education involved, he'd never have been an artist. Once you got into art school, you didn't have to do GCEs.'

If Keith Richards was thus accepted too, he could keep that most noxious of human phenomena, a decision about the future, on hold, allowing the growth of an *idée fixe* that he might make his way in the world as some sort of musician.

2 The Art Student

'There was an incredible electricity in the air, and all the barriers came down – between classical music, jazz and pop and everything else. The band that ended up being the Stones used to practice pure R&B in the breaks, and all the students and staff would go and listen.'

– John Sturgess [1]

During Keith's final weeks at Dartford Technical School, it wasn't all smiles at home either. Doris and Bert's marriage had floated into a sea so stormy that separation was not an 'if' but a 'when'. An unhappy espousal was to muddle on until Bert was almost permanently away from Spielman Road. After his final departure in October 1962, meetings with his wife and son became so increasingly infrequent that they were soon non-existent.

Bert wasn't particularly proud of Keith. To the ordinary working man, whether navvy or ledger clerk, 'art' wasn't a man's trade somehow. For a start, it had doubtful practical value. Put crudely, it was all right as a hobby, but could you rely on it to make a living? If you shone at art in class, it was often treated as a regrettable eccentricity. Your former teachers and fellow ex-pupils alike would shake their heads when they saw you entering art college portals, almost as if they were watching a funeral cortège. Phil May would recall that, 'The last six months of secondary school before that were pretty weird. The masters barely spoke to me – as if going to art college was something to be ashamed of.'

Within four years, May was to grope at the brittle fabric of Top 20 fame as singer with The Pretty Things. It is intriguing to tally how many groups from every strata of mid-1960s pop had roots in art schools. Both The Rolling Stones and The Pretty Things were hatched in Sidcup Art College just as The Rockin' Berries, The Beatles, The Animals, The Kinks, The Yardbirds, The Creation, The Bonzo Dog Doo-Dah Band, The Move, Pentangle and Pink Floyd were in like establishments all over the kingdom.

Guitar hero-in-waiting Jeff Beck was on a two-year course at Wimbledon even as he twanged the wires for The Crescents, a quartet that imitated The Shadows – who functioned as backing combo to Cliff Richard, Tommy Steele's successor as the English Elvis, while notching up instrumental hits in their own right. In the neighbouring town of Kingston, Pentangle's John Renbourn and future Yardbirds Keith Relf, Eric Clapton and Jimmy Page also honed their musical skills in an atmosphere of coloured dust, palette-knives, hammer and chisel and lumpy impasto.

How easy it is to forget that tight-trousered lead vocalist or that clenched-teeth guitarist may have once thus aspired to fine art with music simply an extra-mural pursuit for a dressed-down 'existentialist' with a 'nothing matters' engrossment with self-immolation and death, and 'cool' defined less by Gene Vincent than Amedeo Modigliani.

At Sidcup, Keith Richards distanced himself from the snootier undergraduates by not being self-depreciating about his knowledge and love of rock 'n' roll, even though most of its practitioners were either dead (Buddy Holly), disgraced (Jerry Lee Lewis), in holy orders (Little Richard) or otherwise obsolete. The Everly Brothers were less than a year off enlisting as marines when Elvis completed his own patriotic chore in the US army as a sergeant and 'all-round family entertainer'.

As for Chuck Berry, in 1959, he had served the first of two jail terms that would put temporary halts to his career.

Nevertheless, this incarceration only boosted his cult celebrity in Britain now that its weekly hit parades were heaving with insipidly handsome US boys-next-door, all doe-eyes, hairspray and bashful half-smiles, matched by their forenames (mainly Bobby) and piddle-de-pat records. If they faltered after a brace of chart strikes, queuing round the block would be any number of substitute Bobbies – or Jimmies or Frankies – raring to sing any piffle put in front of them, just like British opposite numbers such as Ronnie Carroll and Mark Wynter with ballads that your mum liked.

Another indication of stagnation was dance-craze records. Little dates an early 1960s film more than the obligatory Twist sequence after this 'most vulgar dance ever invented'[2] emerged as the latest rave worldwide. Its Mecca was New York's Peppermint Lounge, where, to the sound of Joey Dee And The Starliters, socialites and middle-aged trendsetters mingled with beatniks to do the Twist, in which you pretended to towel your back while grinding out a cigarette butt with your foot. Worse, it wouldn't go away, probably because you were too spoilt for choice with alternatives such as the Fly, the Jerk, the Locomotion, the Slop, the Mashed Potato, the ungainly Turkey Trot, the Mickey's Monkey, the Hitch-Hiker, the back-breaking Limbo, the Hully Gully, the Madison – and even a revival of the Charleston commensurate with a resurgence of traditional jazz so pronounced that Acker Bilk, Chris Barber, Kenny Ball and several more of its British practitioners became chart contenders.

In this desert of Bobbies, Twist variations and Bilk's million-selling 'Stranger On The Shore', there were scattered oases. Joey Dee's 'Peppermint Twist' was actually quite enthralling – while Ray Charles's 'Hit The Road Jack' in 1961 traded call-and-response with his female vocal trio, The Raelettes, like a spiritual's exhorter–congregation interplay. Of like persuasion, The Marvelettes' 'Please Mr Postman' and Barrett Strong's 'Money' were among the first fistful of entries for Tamla-

Motown, a promising black label from Detroit, in what US compilers had just stopped styling the 'sepia' charts.

Such discs, and others from untold North American independent companies, were either taped from sources like the US Forces Network or else wended across the Atlantic by means as mysterious as a particular brand of footwear had to St Kilda, the most remote Hebridean island, barely a year after its appearance in Victorian London. Often desirable for their very obscurity, many of these items were spun time and time again on the turntable at Sidcup College of Art's Music Society gatherings – initially, no more than record-playing sessions – after lectures on Fridays.

One evening, someone brought in 1958's 'I Put A Spell On You' by Screamin' Jay Hawkins, who, so listening students understood, was a macabre black Elvis from Ohio. It had been his inspired notion to have aides drop handfuls of rubber bands from the gallery and stage-whisper 'Worms!' during an act that commenced with Jay's slow and sulphurous emergence from a coffin bathed in eerie fluorescence. Garbed in perhaps a turban, zebra-striped formal attire and pink cloak, he would produce props like a cigarette-puffing skull mounted on a stick and an array of powdery potions, while he swooped from warbling mock-operatics, half-spoken recitative, low grumbles – 'wurrrrrr' – and insane falsetto shrieks.

After years of a thankless slog of one-nighters and flop singles, he'd struck gold with 'I Put A Spell On You'. With the best of intentions, he'd bustled into the studio with a light romantic ditty that might have suited Nat 'King' Cole. The recording wasn't going very well, and some liquor was procured to loosen the tension. Several takes later, the song had mutated into the goggle-eyed ravings of a man so drunk he was recording flat on his back.

By fair means or foul, Keith had to have 'I Put A Spell On You', just as he had to have Chuck Berry's latest – 'Let It Rock'

– and those by artists he'd discovered via credits and sleeve notes on Berry LPs and further points of reference, such as Elvis Presley's debt to Arthur 'Big Boy' Crudup, also a resident of the blues capital of Memphis in the early 1950s. Presley's first regional hit was to be a cover of 'That's Alright Mama' by Crudup, who was to pass away in 1974 still awaiting a fat royalty cheque via the King.

Less specifically, Keith had learned that, in the decades that preceded rock 'n' roll, a white radio listener in the United States might have tuned in by accident to muffled bursts of what segregationist pamphlets denigrated as 'screaming idiotic words and savage music' on some Negro-run station – and that it had been possible for the likes of Arthur Crudup to score in the US 'sepia' – or 'rhythm-and-blues' as it became – charts without figuring at all in the parallel dimensions of the corresponding country-and-western tabulation and the pop *Hot 100*.

That had been how John Lee Hooker's 'I'm In The Mood' and 'Boogie Chillun' had each been registered as million-sellers in 1948. Though these, and later discs stamped with the same droning blues-boogie undercurrent, were available only on import, Hooker's was a name to drop at Sidcup Art College along with those of Elmore James – whose 'Rollin' And Tumblin'' was to be a blues 'standard' – and his mentor Robert Johnson, a bluesman tormented by an inferno of ectoplasmic monsters.

The most obsessed of his exorcisms in this vein, 'Me And The Devil Blues', was taped in 1937, a few months before Johnson's slow death by poison at the age of 24. For all his youth, there are those – such as noted pop critic Charles Shaar Murray – who reckon poor Robert was the greatest musician ever to have walked the planet. Keith Richards wouldn't go that far, but he was to avow that 'if Robert Johnson had lived into the era of electric guitar, he'd have killed us all. When you listen to him, the cat's got Bach going on down low and Mozart going on up high. The cat was counterpointing.'[3]

Johnson's records had proved as instructional years previously to Muddy Waters, whose in-concert *Muddy Waters At Newport* album obtained a UK release in 1960. Seen by Richards as the missing link between Johnson and Berry, Waters had been taking the stage with an electric six-string and, also amid much criticism from blues purists, lewd pelvic movements akin to those of Presley. What more did he need to earn the admiration of one such as Keith – whose vision was shared with other students, some of whom joined him in attempts to reproduce the black sounds themselves? 'There were jam sessions in the cloakroom with Keith, Dick Taylor and me,' affirmed Phil May, 'We wanted something that was ours, Muddy Waters, John Lee Hooker, Bo Diddley and so on – as we didn't like trad jazz, Acker Bilk, Kenny Ball and all that stuff.'

From Dartford Grammar School, Dick Taylor was an academic year above Richards and the younger May. What drew them together was guitars. Both Dick and Keith possessed models with electronic pick-ups – and, compared to his first guitar, Keith's Hofner Futurama cutaway was as a fountain pen to a stub of pencil. When they began practising together, both Taylor's fretboard expertise and his theoretical insight impressed Richards.

Subsequent conversations also brought forth the information that Dick's grandfather, like Theodore Augustus Dupree, had mastered many instruments. These included the drums set up in the Taylor home in Bexleyheath. Dick's own mastery of the kit had attracted overtures for his services from several groups in the Medway valley where it was given that, rather than playing the crazy, far-out music that intrigued Sidcup art collegians, reputations were made doling out assembly-line Bobby-ish pop in parochial ballrooms, halfway houses between amateur bashes in the local youth club, commandeered lecture theatres or the back room of the Cat-and-Paintbrush and nationwide 'scream circuit' tours – with recording contracts a far-fetched afterthought.

In about 1961 the prongs of a triumvirate that ruled pop in northwest Kent were: Erkey Grant And His Tonettes; Terry Lee And The Checkers, pride of Orpington; and, Eltham's 'answer' to Cliff Richard And The Shadows, Bern Elliott And The Fenmen – named after the Jolly Fenman pub where, fresh out of school in 1960, the personnel had been regulars. The Fenmen's *forte* was, however, not Shadowy instrumentals but a breathtaking four-part vocal harmony behind hip-shakin' Bern. 'We used to go and watch them,' recalled Phil May, 'but we would wait for them to play their two Chuck Berry numbers. The best English R&B band was Johnny Kidd And The Pirates. I remember going with Dick to Blackheath purely to see them because they were one of few English ballroom bands to actually have R&B roots.'

Yet, for all their preoccupation with music, May's and Taylor's lecture notebooks were as conscientiously full as Richards' were empty. When written or practical assessment was pending, he'd cadge assistance just as he would a cigarette. 'It was obvious from the beginning that Keith was on the course so as not to have to get a job,' observed Phil. 'He had no real interest in graphics. His work certainly wasn't very good.'

His tutors could not help but imagine that Keith did very little interrelated reading, and that, when drawn from deep silence, he bluffed his way through prolonged discussion on art. His bluff was called sometimes by graphics lecturer John Sturgess, whose strategies would be unorthodox even now. Phil May's recollections leave little doubt that in a more strait-laced cultural era, Sturgess's methodology may have been seen as verging on lunacy: 'I remember one life-drawing class. I was a very naive 15-year-old, standing there, looking at this naked person, and I couldn't put a mark down. John gave me two bob and told me to go down the pub, have half a pint and come back when I had something to say. He was fantastic like that.

'John put Stravinsky on during lessons, and turned me onto classical music. He was also to be very tolerant about The Pretty Things. We'd tell him we were gigging, and he'd say we could leave at 3pm and come in early the next day. So we'd come in at noon the next day, but we'd work till midnight. The print room was only open from nine to five, so John told us to get ourselves locked in and climb out of the window. He hijacked the education system and said, "These are your facilities. You're not at normal school. This is your time." Our year contained a lot of talent. That gave us a lot of respect from older students. We were supposed to be doing graphic design, but we got into painting and not so much lavatory-roll adverts'.

Sturgess was either unaware or turned a blind eye to further rule-bending such as John Stax, The Pretty Things' bass player, impersonating a new student for the best part of a term, and, more sinister, the use of stimulants other than beer to, say, steady nerves for sketching a nude. Dick, Keith and Phil had already been introduced to the early 1960s equivalent of glue-sniffing – buying a Vicks inhaler from the chemist's and isolating that part of it that contained an excitant called benzedrine, which would then be eaten. It was a tacky way of getting 'high', but it was the nearest you could get to sharing something with musical icons inspired by the partaking of drugs outlawed for recreational purposes. Cocaine was mentioned in 'I Get A Kick Out Of You' by Cole Porter, and amphetamines were the subject of Bo Diddley's 'Pills' long before pop stars and drugs became as Tweedledum to Tweedledee in newspaper headlines.

Keith would blame his profound dependency in later life to narcotics on their being 'passed from one generation of musicians to the next'. [4] For an impressionable youth like him, musical credibility seemed to be enhanced if you had some kind of addiction. Look at Hank Williams, whose substance abuse had killed him. Ray Charles mainlined on heroin and, closer to home, a bloke called Cyril Davies was to collapse and die on stage, thanks to alcoholism aggravating his residual leukaemia. Unknown then to the Sidcup blues enthusiasts, mouth-organist and blues shouter Davies was in the process of forming Britain's first electric blues band with guitarist Alexis Korner, also in his 30s and a former traditional jazzman.

After lending a sour ear to the young Korner playing boogie-woogie on the front-room piano, his father had locked the lid and kept the key about his person. Shortly after this incident, Alexis, deemed to be 'disturbed', had been packed off to Finchden Manor, a therapeutic community for such boys in the Weald of Kent. Like film actor James Robertson Justice and post-punk pop star Tom Robinson, he was one of Finchden's success stories.

Keith Richards, however, was to be the most notorious Old Boy of Sidcup Art College. His career there was soon tracing the same dismaying trajectory as it had at Dartford Technical School. Failure seemed inevitable from the beginning. By the middle of his second year on the graphics course he, his parents and the college staff acknowledged tacitly that his higher education studies were unofficially over and that the ugly moment was approaching when he'd have to find a 'proper job' to keep alive.

As it turned out, the only paid work Keith Richards ever did, apart from as a musician, was as a Saturday boy in a local supermarket – and as a relief postman during 1961's Christmas recess for just long enough for the novelty of the early mornings not to be too onerous. Then there was doubtful speculation about him becoming, perhaps, a jobbing commercial artist, a copywriter in 'the big, wide world of advertising, full-time'[5] or, via a supplicatory chat with John Sturgess, a departmental technician back at the college.

It wasn't immediate, but all such plans, realistic or otherwise, were to recede into the background after Keith experienced one of those Momentous Encounters one morning on the commuter train from Dartford to Sidcup.

3 The Fellow Traveller

'Back in 1962, starting a blues band was not the way to
stardom.'
                                                    – *Keith Richards*[1]

It was a triviality that changed Keith Richards' life. At Dartford
railway station, the sun peeped through gaps in the cloudy
October sky and an elderly road sweeper pushed a broom along
the gutter near the taxi rank as Keith sauntered past the
newspaper stand with its chalked headline from the *Kentish
Times*. The train was just pulling in, and it was by the merest
chance that Richards, drifting like a ghost through the steam
hissing from the undercarriage, entered the same section and slid
open the door of the same dusty second-class compartment
where Mick Jagger, on a degree course at the London School of
Economics (LSE), was already seated.

They nodded in vague recognition of each other as increasing
sunshine gleamed where it could through the grime-encrusted
window. On and off, casual paths had crossed since both had
attended Wentworth Primary where Jagger, whose birthday was
late in the summer term, had been in the year above Richards,
though only a few months separated them.

During the stop–start journey, with its slow embarkations
from Bexley, Albany Park, Barnehurst and the rest of the
lugubrious London boroughs that preceded Sidcup, began one of
the most crucial liaisons in pop. Jagger and Richards might have
exchanged hardly a single sentence had not Keith glimpsed
Chuck Berry's *Rocking At The Hop* on top of a pile of five LPs

that Mick had under his arm. With some astonishment, he asked about this black beauty, which was obtainable only on import. Keith could understand perfectly why someone might give up five years of his life to own that record.

Of ensuing remarks that weren't directly to do with *Rocking At The Hop*, *The Best Of Muddy Waters* and Mick's other albums, it transpired that they had a mutual friend in Dick Taylor, who, just as he had been with Phil May and Keith at the art college, was mucking about on guitars with Mick and some other friends from the Grammar. They called themselves 'Little Boy Blue And The Blue Boys'. Why didn't Keith bring his Hofner along to the next rehearsal?

As the group had an embarrassment of guitarists, most of them just strumming chords, Mick – as Phil May was to do during the cloakroom sessions – elected to leave his instrument at home so that he could concentrate on lead vocals. For an audible but private gauge of how they sounded with Keith in the ranks, a Grundig tape recorder was to be rigged up in the most acoustically sympathetic corner of somebody's bedroom or shed, possibly at Spielman Road. After much fiddling with microphone positioning as the valves warmed up, the lads committed 15 pieces to reel-to-reel – among them no less than six Berry items plus 'You're Right I'm Left She's Gone', Bo Diddley's 'You Can't Judge A Book By The Cover' and other songs regarded as harsh throwbacks now that pop was at its most harmless and ephemeral.[2]

Little Boy Blue And The Blue Boys, however, were never more than a bunch of lads playing together for the hell of it. They were amateurs with no other aim than 'to turn people onto the blues,' outlined Keith, 'If we could turn them onto Muddy, Jimmy Reed, Howlin' Wolf and John Lee Hooker, then our job was done.'[3] To this end, they had the impact of a feather on concrete, working up an involuntary audience of their own families – and neighbours complaining that the volume of the rehearsals was getting beyond a joke, especially after the nth false start of 'Johnny B Goode'.

No Blue Boy felt that he had either the knack or the inclination to make up a song himself. In any case, it might have invited howls of affectionate derision and hectoring arguments along the lines of 'You can't beat the Yanks at that game anymore than you can at anything else,' or, 'We don't need more than what we're playing already. If we did, could a twit like you come up with anything of the necessary standard?'

Quite aside from the group's own thoughts, a lingering prejudice of most British record companies in the early 1960s was that the last thing anyone from a teenager in a dancehall to the head of the Light Programme wanted to hear was a home-made song. The notion of anyone in a pop group developing composition to any marked extent had been unheard of until 1958 when, on the bus en route to the studio, guitarist Ian Samwell penned 'Move It', Cliff Richard's chart breakthrough. Though hastily recorded and in artistic debt to Chuck Berry, it still ranks – with the likes of Johnny Kidd's 'Please Don't Touch' and Vince Taylor's 'Brand New Cadillac' – as one of few classic British rock 'n' roll singles from an age when the typical UK pop entertainer accepted his second-hand and, arguably, counterfeit status to US role models.

That was also the attitude of Blues Incorporated, house band at the now-celebrated G Club on Ealing Broadway, not far from Bert Richards' factory. Both the combo and the venue were manifestations of Cyril Davies' and Alexis Korner's crusade on behalf of the British blues movement. On the first evening – 17 May 1962 – the set covered all waterfronts from 'How Long How Long', a skiffle stand-by originated in the Mississippi delta in the 1930s, to '(Get Your Kicks On) Route 66', which, if old enough to be recorded in 1952 by Nat 'King' Cole,[4] was a staple of Chuck Berry's stage act and thus an opus that stretched the envelope of what was deemed to be blues by one such as Cyril

Davies, whose preference for a narrower interpretation led him eventually to form a splinter group, The All-Stars, and found a breakaway club in Harrow-on-the-Hill.

Policy disagreements were, however, not yet out in the open when Little Boy Blue And The Blue Boys organised a crowded trip in Mick's father's car to sample a night at the G Club. Temporary brake failure had them accelerating down a hill towards a level crossing, but this near-disaster did not deflect them from their iron purpose.

In the first instance, it was enough that Blues Incorporated and its stamping ground even existed. However, it seemed to be better to travel than arrive – because it was already over somehow as the party from Dartford trooped across the opaque paving windows and down the worn stairwell into the enveloping fug and sticky heat. Only a miracle could have stopped them feeling a sense of anti-climax. It was like expecting a drop-handlebarred racing bike for your birthday but getting a sensibly huff-puff sit-up-and-beg with no gears.

Yet Blues Incorporated didn't consist entirely of hoary old troupers from trad jazz. Furthermore, even if it had, a lot of Keith, Mick *et al*'s black heroes were married, middle-aged, bald and obese too, but they were the genuine article, weren't they? It wasn't quite the same equation as Hal Burton to The Crickets – mundane Embassy to exotic Coral – nor a sort of inverted colour prejudice, but Alexis, Cyril and the other blokes were a bit too pat, too dovetailed, too English.

While familiarity didn't breed contempt, having ascertained the situation, Jagger – and then the less assertive Richards and Taylor – joined a queue of guest musicians from the audience, not caring who they disconcerted by giving 'em 'Reelin' And Rockin'', 'Roll Over Beethoven' and further rock 'n' roll. Some of the fellows and Keith also started visiting the affable Korner's house in Bayswater to talk music on the afternoons before the G Club. Phonetically pliant, Richards' tongue slipped easily into Korner's hip, pseudo-transatlantic vocabulary, inserting 'man' into sentences where 'mate' had once been. He also got used to referring to females as 'chicks' and men as 'cats'. As appealing was Korner's speaking voice, a smoky drawl with a seasoning of the officer-and-gentleman.

Striving perhaps not to put his foot in it with some inanity Keith, more often than not, decided it was safer to draw on a reticent cigarette and nod in smiling agreement with whoever had spoken last. 'At first, you got the impression that Keith was just trailing around with Mick,' thought Korner, 'but it didn't take long to realise that Keith wasn't trailing around at all. He just happened to be quieter.'[5]

They were now mighty close, Keith and Mick. The personal dynamic between them would be such that, while they weren't exactly David and Jonathan, no other man would know Jagger as intimately as Richards, not even his own younger brother. Behind the public intimacies of off-mike comments and momentary eye-contacts over the subsequent decades, there were jokes side-splitting to nobody else; Mick's heart feeling like it would burst through his ribcage when Keith smiled at him; abrupt reconciliations after hours of verbal and emotional baiting and the hidden implication in a seemingly innocuous remark sparking off a hastily unplugged guitar and a slammed backstage fire exit.

Expressions of love (and hatred) between heterosexual men can frequently be boorish, but, nonetheless, sincere. In an Andy Capp cartoon in the *Daily Mirror*, Capp – a beer-swilling, womanising Geordie – is dissecting the character of his best pal, Chalky, over a venomous pint. A chap on the next bar stool adds a disobliging remark of his own about Chalky. Capp's response is not grim agreement but an uppercut that sends the other sprawling: 'That's my mate you're talking about!'

As solid a bedrock of the rapport between Keith and Mick was the potential of each to outfit the other with vestments of personality he had desired but never before dared to wear. For all his workin' class 'ero affectations, Mick knew how he was supposed to behave in accordance with his privet-hedged upbringing in the better part of Dartford. Conversely, despite his fascination with Alexis Korner's accent and genteel bearing, Keith didn't need to brutalise himself to facilitate a 'common touch' when what was left of Little Boy Blue And The Blue Boys began performing to audiences less sympathetic than those in the G Club.

Everyone but Keith, Dick and Mick had fallen by the wayside by 1962's cold spring when an amalgamation with two mainstays of another nascent group took place. They were an unlikely pair. Belying an assumed reposeful cool, Brian Jones had barred a fiery 'bottleneck' guitar one night at the G Club. Likewise, both his ruthless ambition and a self-promoted reputation as a devil with women were at odds with his girly enunciation and camp mannerisms. As 'gay' is now, 'musical' was once a euphemism for 'homosexual'. Brian, however, was musical by original definition only – with an instinct for deriving melody or rhythm from virtually any object put in front of him, whether a blade of grass, the most complicated electronic keyboard or the proverbial kitchen sink.

By contrast, Ian 'Stu' Stewart restricted himself to piano. On auto-pilot, his left hand would roll a fast and circular boogie-woogie bass while the right skipped up and down the higher keys in 'barrelhouse' fashion with a touch that ranged from the utmost delicacy to muscle-bound force, just like Jelly Roll Morton, Little Brother Montgomery, Pinetop Smith and other ancient black masters of the idiom.

Stewart was also as ostensibly manly as Jones wasn't. A sweaty aptitude for athletics had wrought in Ian a sturdy rather than slim physique. He also had a rugged, lantern-jawed face on which craggy eyebrows jutted from a forehead topped by a slicked-back smarm of a haircut. 'He'd wear these ludicrous black leather shorts,' grinned Keith, 'and always ride a bicycle. When we rehearsed, Stu would be looking out the window to make sure his bike was still there – but he'd always hit the right notes.'[5]

While all Ian and the others had in common – socially as well as musically – consolidated a growing friendship, so equally did the differences between them. 'Basically, I come from the same sort of background as Brian and Mick,' explained Stewart, 'middle class and fairly well-educated. I'd never really been exposed to anyone like Keith before. He was a complete layabout.'[5]

Unlike Stewart and, for a while, Jones, no obligations to regular employment hindered Taylor, Richards and Jagger's availability for the bookings that, hopefully, were to pour in after the group made its stage debut – billed as 'The Rolling Stones' in a *Jazz News* preview[6] – on a summer Thursday at the Marquee in the middle of London, with a pick-up drummer and a set-list that walked an uncomfortable line between reassuringly familiar G Club crowd-pleasers and Chuck Berry. Some onlookers voiced their scorn for the callow – and, these days, increasingly more prevalent – impudence of superimposing rock 'n' roll on the blues grid – as instanced too by Taylor plucking an electric bass guitar rather than the acoustic double bass that made Blues Incorporated more 'authentic'.

'I was out my tree on benzedrine,' confessed Dick, 'and it put me off it forever.' He was to become disgruntled too about the mere handful of engagements that had followed the Marquee debut, some self-financed, in community institutes used more frequently for amateur dramatics and table tennis. Into the bargain, it was clear that rhythm and blues was on a par with jazz as 'starvation music'. It occurred to Taylor that he stood more chance of a livelihood as an artist than as a musician, and, with a scholarship at the Central School of Art on offer, he told Brian, Ian, Mick and Keith to look for a replacement.

Though Keith had acquired a Harmony Meteor semi-acoustic – an improvement on the Hofner – on aggregate, an individual Stone's income was a fraction of that of the counter assistant at the café near Notting Hill Gate tube station where Keith and one or two of the others would congregate sometimes. 'One day, Brian and I met Mick and Keith there,' remembered Pat Andrews, Jones' then-girlfriend, 'Mick – whose student grant cheque had just come in – bought us a mixed grill, and Brian and my diets did not extend to that.

'Keith was very quiet most of the time. He was to portray himself as being a hard, street-wise bad boy, but he came across as exactly the opposite. Keith was a mummy's boy. He wasn't a womaniser at all. Music was his life. He idolised Brian then because his own repertoire was very limited – more or less just Chuck Berry.'

Pat was also witness to the shifts in the group's power structure whereby Ian Stewart was to be marginalised eventually, and a mutable high command of Richards, Jones and Jagger established. 'It started off with Mick and Keith,' noted Pat, 'Then it was Mick and Brian, and then Keith and Brian.'

As it had been with Keith and Dick in Sidcup, guitars were the common denominator between Brian and Keith. The often breathtaking instrumental passages onstage were as much duets as solos, with less emphasis on improvising over chord sequences than predetermined construction to integrate with the melodic and lyrical intent of a given number. Like Scotty Moore's 'Hound Dog' break, certain transcendental moments on the boards (and, later, on disc) would look impossible if transcribed on manuscript paper. 'It was Brian and I who'd really got into the essence of this two guitar thing,' recounted Richards, 'Of trying to get them to go into each other – and you wouldn't care particularly who suddenly flew out and did a little line, and that you could almost read each others' mind.'[5]

Depending on your point of view, Keith and Brian's fingered concord seemed either anodyne or attractively unfussed against the grimacing flash of would-be guitar virtuosi like high-speed Alvin Dean[7] of Nottingham's Jaybirds, Stan Webb of Kidderminster's Shades Five or Frank White, the first British owner of a twin-necked Gibson, in Jimmy Crawford And The Ravens, Sheffield's boss group.

The latter outfit had shown what was possible in late 1961 when, after landing a recording contract with EMI subsidiary, Columbia – Cliff Richard's label, which didn't include The Ravens, Crawford scored in the Top 20 with a US cover, 'I Love How You Love Me'. That, however, was that as far as the British record-buying public was concerned for Jimmy and his boys. Nevertheless, they were to remain key personalities whose activities – professional and otherwise – were chronicled, along with venue information, in *Top Star Special*, a supplement of the *Sheffield Star*. The very existence too of *Mersey Beat*, *Midland Beat* and Torquay-based *South-West Scene*, to name but three similar journals, would also demonstrate the depth and cohesion of local pop scenes of which few outside a designated region were aware.

'We had no idea about what was going on in Liverpool, for example,' affirmed Keith Richards.[8] Sticking with Sheffield as a case study, a veritable host of outfits ruled specific vicinities in the Steel City as Cliff Richard And The Shadows did the national hit parade. Now that hard-nosed entrepreneurs had smelled the money to be made, of net takings of £60 at, say, St Aidan's Church Hall, less than a third of that would be split between maybe three groups who were happy just to have somewhere to make their racket. With some of them trading in the same kind of music as The Rolling Stones, so began the careers of Johnny Hawk And His Falcons, The Steve Denton Group, Tony Gale And The Stormers, Dean Marshall And His Deputies, Vince Young And The Vantennas, Peter York And His Pontiacs, Alan B Curtis And The Tumblers, The Scott William Combo, Pete

Emmett And The Skyliners, Dave Berry And The Cruisers, Mark Stone And The Questors, Vance Arnold And The Avengers, Mickey's Monkeys, Small Paul And His Young Ones, the immaculately attired Pete Fender Show and Johnny Tempest And His Cadillacs. A random selection of those without a singing non-instrumentalist to the fore are The Classics, The Kodiaks, The Staggerlees, The Originators, Ye Thimbleriggers, Zakkery Thak, The Saville Row Rhythm Unit, The Lizards, The Chicago Line, the sober-suited Citizens, The Male Set and The Square Circles. Even Sheffield's Polish community could boast a group; Tempo Four.

By 1963 nearly all of them would exemplify the two guitars-bass-drums that was to be the archetype of the British beat explosion – as did The Cherokees, who held Ventnor's 69 Club on the Isle of Wight as Kerry Rapid And The Blue Stars did Aldershot's Central ballroom; Pete Mystery And His Strangers did the village halls surrounding Andover; The Rockin' Berries, Yardley's Twitch Club; The Beatles, the Cavern in Liverpool; Bern Elliott And The Fenmen, Dartford's Railway Tavern; The Cossacks and The Jaguars, tussling over Thursday nights at Worcester's 'Ot Spot, and The Golden Crusaders, the Plaza in Belfast.

From January 1963, The Rolling Stones presided over Sundays at the Craw Daddy in the back of Richmond's Station Hotel after rhythm and blues had come to Surrey in the form of The Dave Hunt Band, who specialised in Louis Jordan-style jump-blues. One snow-flecked afternoon, Hunt rang Craw Daddy proprietor Georgio Gomelsky, a White Russian who had lived in Germany, Italy and Switzerland, to say that he and his group couldn't make it. Via Ian Stewart's telephone at his place of work, Gomelsky told the Stones that, as long as they didn't turn up with only half their equipment or a player short, the gig was theirs.

This try out was promising enough for Gomelsky to not only offer a residency, but 'divide the door receipts each Sunday equally with them'.[9] Next, a date schedule that had once signified a month's work became a week's. 'At the time, we thought the absolute pinnacle of success would be maybe three or four regular gigs in London,' guffawed Keith.[10] Nevertheless, you'd still see him, Mick and Brian mooching around the city centre, calculating what the one-shilling-and-sevenpence-halfpenny between them would do. A plate of beans on toast washed down with a cup of liquid smoke from a snack bar on the Embankment? It was as if they'd never invoked sporadic screams from a few girls in the Craw Daddy for a particularly bravura 'Roll Over Beethoven' or shelled out for an hour at the Curly Clayton Sound Studio in north London, albeit bunched round an omni-directional microphone and with no bass player.

Purportedly, Brian – who tended to be singled out as 'leader' – was so impoverished that he swapped one of the resulting acetates for an article of clothing. Yet, though he had a child by Pat to support, and vocational caution kept Mick at the LSE, the two of them plus Keith elected to rent a flat together so that they could more easily attend to Stones matters.

Once it might have been the acme of elegance with its bay windows and the pillars supporting the front porch, but 102 Edith Grove, SW10, a stone's throw from the Thames, was now divided into bedsits that might be described by an estate agent as 'compact'. Their various states of disrepair were expressed to passers-by in peeling paintwork, leaking gutters, ledges off-white with pigeon droppings and rubbish sogging behind railings. Inside, there was no adequate sanitation or central heating. The entire terrace in which No. 102 stood seemed to shiver as underground trains clattered along the three Circle and District line tracks that connected at Earl's Court.

'Oh man, it was filthy,' exclaimed Keith, 'We just starved and listened to the blues, and played all day.'[9] It was beyond them to give the place a quick flick round with a duster when all the 'O's' on the front page of yesterday's *Daily Sketch* had to be filled in.

'They'd stay in bed all day,' moped Doris Richards, 'because they had no money for the heater, food or anything.'[5]

During a severe spell of blizzards in the dying days of 1962, Keith woke up so headachy and fevered that he went home to mother – though in the teeth of her worry, he dragged himself from a huddle of bedclothes to honour the next evening's date at the Piccadilly Jazz Club where The Rolling Stones were third on the bill to Blues Incorporated.

4 Cliff's Brother

'Keith doesn't like anyone to think he's shy. He opposes that by being over-confident. Actually, the more I get to know Keith, the shyer he seems to be.'

– Bill Wyman [1]

By January 1963, the classic Rolling Stones line-up had found each other. Sharing the Craw Daddy stage with Keith, Mick, Brian and Ian were two Londoners: drummer Charlie Watts, once of Blues Incorporated, and bass player Bill Wyman, towards whom Richards was, initially, civil but not over-friendly. The new recruit was, however, willing to assist in singing harmonies and responses behind Jagger. Though the Stones had the confidence to both play and, eventually, compose derivative instrumentals, the Merseybeat craze, spearheaded by The Beatles, placed a stronger emphasis on vocals and the idea that someone like Mick was an integral part of the group rather than singled out as a separate entity as Cliff Richard was from The Shadows or Bern Elliott from The Fenmen.

In the first instance, Keith shied away from the microphone. Partly it was because the choirboy in him was dejected by having to virtually gulp it when straining to hear himself through puny public-address systems in the days before onstage monitors. He'd been finicky about pitch from earliest youth during 'musical evenings' at his grandfather's. 'If I didn't sing a grace note,' remembered his mother, 'Keith would tell me to do it properly. He'd know it was wrong. It's something that's just built into him.' [1]

Jump-cutting to the Craw Daddy, Studio 51 – a basement off Covent Garden[2] – and other venues in and around London where the Stones worked from the beginning of 1963 to the late spring, it wasn't worth being too fussy about casually strewn vocal mistakes. Besides, The Beatles were a hard yardstick in that department for any group. 'Keith liked them because he was quite interested in their chord sequences,' said Mick, 'He also liked their harmonies, which were always a problem with The Rolling Stones. Keith always tried to get the harmonies off the ground, but they always seemed messy.'[1]

Scouse was now the most romantic dialect in the country, and was to be represented at the *New Musical Express* Pollwinners concert at Wembley Pool on 21 April by Gerry And The Pacemakers as well as The Beatles – whose own John Lennon and Paul McCartney had written each side of all three of their hit singles. The riptide of Merseybeat was about to overwhelm other acts on the bill: The Springfields, Frank Ifield, Adam Faith, Mark Wynter, The Tornados, The Brook Brothers ('Britain's *ace* vocal group', according to a 1962 press hand-out), Billy Fury – and even Cliff Richard And The Shadows. They and, to a lesser extent, Adam and Billy would weather the deluge, and Dusty, The Springfields' panda-eyed glamour puss, would achieve spectacular solo success, but, within 18 months, the rest would be performing in venues where current chart standing had no meaning.

By then, Britain would be the planet's prime purveyor of pop, thanks to self-contained beat groups that were no longer apeing their North American cousins. Rather than mechanical mimicking, the intention was to make 'Money', 'Poison Ivy', 'Fortune Teller', 'Do You Love Me', 'Walking The Dog', 'If You Gotta Make A Fool Of Somebody' and other of what had become R&B 'standards' sound different from not only the US templates, but also any other domestic outfit's arrangement. Hence The Animals' workmanlike renderings of Bo Diddley's 'Mona' and Larry Williams's 'She Said Yeah', and the Stones' more dulcet and echo-laden crack at the former and frantic work-out of the latter, just one step from chaos. Also, though The Animals' Alan Price could crush notes with the best of them, another crucial factor was his keyboard's purer tone and fixed tuning lacking the essential dissonance at the rough guitar heart of R&B.

A healthier indication of the acceptance of native characteristics than simply rifling US vaults was that if a group attempted a self-penned song, it wasn't necessarily an unofficial intermission so that palais audiences could talk to friends, get in a round of drinks, go to the toilets, anything but dance or even listen to it. However, after the gift of a Lennon-McCartney opus became like a licence to print banknotes, the pair would still be damned by a *Sunday Times* critic in 1966 with such faint praise as 'reasonably good "amateur" composers, greatly assisted by the poverty of British composing standards';[3] this, three years after every original track on *With The Beatles* had been covered by another artist, whether 'Little Child' by a Billy Fonteyne, 'All My Loving' by The Dowlands – or 'I Wanna Be Your Man' as The Rolling Stones' second single.

'Pop music then was so undervalued by adults,' sighed Tom Robinson, then a 14-year-old with *The Five Faces Of Manfred Mann* LP on instant replay on his Dansette, 'They weren't aware that legendary times were taking place. Maybe that's what's happening today with boy bands and hip-hop. Perhaps we're not taking them seriously enough – like the jazz purists didn't the Stones and the Manfreds.'

Genealogically connected to Blues Incorporated too, Manfred Mann were on terms of fluctuating commercial equality with the Stones from summer 1963 into the New Year, during which time both acts issued three 45s. While the Stones' chart success was more immediate, Manfred Mann were first into the Top Ten with '54321' while 'I Wanna Be Your Man' was slipping away from its apogee of Number 12.

An earlier signal that journalists were no longer obliged to traipse up north for pop news had been Barking's Brian Poole and the Tremeloes' go at 'Do You Love Me' knocking The Beatles' fourth A-side, 'She Loves You', from Number One in autumn – though it regained its pole position three weeks later. Nevertheless, there was to be another unfair, if jubilant, Fleet Street field day in January 1964 when Tottenham's Dave Clark Five unseated Lennon *et al*'s unbroken seven weeks at the top after failed attempts by Cliff, Dusty Springfield – and Manchester's Freddie And The Dreamers. Though they were fronted by a sort of Norman Wisdom of pop, Keith Richards had half-liked their spirited revival of 'If You Gotta Make A Fool Of Somebody'. Freddie himself preferred the James Ray original of 1961, but this R&B singalong suited his Gerry-with-a-hernia voice and the tempo of his Dreamers' act. All Freddie needed was a spot on ITV's *Thank Your Lucky Stars* on 21 May 1963 for his clowning to nudge the record into the Top Ten.

Six weeks later, the Stones were on the same programme, also miming to their first release. Trying to avoid numbers in the portfolios of scores of other groups, the Stones had listened hard to both the back catalogue and the latest from the R&B mother-lode. Pye had just launched an album series that was bringing many of the old delta and urban legends to a wider public. *Folk Festival Of The Blues*, for example, was an aural souvenir of a Chicago concert the previous summer, showcasing Muddy Waters, Willie Dixon, Sonny Boy Williamson, Buddy Guy and Howlin' Wolf.

High street record shops were also stocking both reissued and new singles such as Bo Diddley's 'Road Runner' (coupled with 'Pretty Thing'), 'Boom Boom' from John Lee Hooker and, the Stones' final choice for their maiden single, Chuck Berry's so-so 'Come On' – 'because it was the most commercial sound we were capable of making at the time,' shrugged Keith, 'and the song had some kind of affinity with what we were used to doing.'[1]

While Chuck Berry's stronger follow-up, 'Memphis Tennessee', would eclipse an arrangement by Dave Berry And The Cruisers, and 1964 held a greater triumph for an unopposed 'No Particular Place To Go', he, Diddley, Hooker, Waters, Wolf and all the rest of them were, overall, less appealing to UK youth than the beat groups who borrowed from them. For most people who didn't derive deep and lasting pleasure from studying composing credits on record labels, The Rolling Stones' 'Come On' was the *only* version.

'I reckon there are three reasons why American R&B stars don't click with British teenage fans,' theorised Keith, 'one, they're old; two, they're black; three, they're ugly.'[1] His not satisfying the ordained physical requirements of a mid-1960s pop star was the chief reason why Ian Stewart did not join the other Stones before the *Thank Your Lucky Stars* cameras – or on any other TV show for the rest of the decade and beyond. After he'd come to terms with this banishment, and his shaving mirror telling him why, Stewart hovered unseen somewhere in the hierarchy between the humblest equipment-humper and the Jagger-Jones-Richards axis. 'He was the glue that held all the bits together,' was to be Keith's epitaph following Ian's death in 1985, 'Very few people realise how important he was to the Stones.'[4] As early as 1964, however, Ian was to be the subject of a *New Musical Express* feature in which he insisted that he was 'happy collecting the odd three farthings that come from the records. I don't want to be pointed out in the street, and get torn to pieces.'[5] It was published a few months after an article in *Melody Maker* about Pete Best, the drummer who was dumped when The Beatles were on point of take off.

Another adjustment when the Stones were in the same position was the truncated surname foisted on Keith. It was to be 'Richard' now, giving him an implied affiliation with Cliff. That a Birmingham combo called The Tempests also contained a guitarist named Keith Richards, however, had not been another consideration when the Stones' first management team, Eric Easton and Andrew Loog Oldham, imposed the change. [6]

Of the two, Oldham was the most instantly impressive, having once been employed briefly by Brian Epstein, manager of The Beatles, Gerry and other chart-busting Merseybeat acts, as a publicist. On closer acquaintance, however, it transpired that, not only was he younger than his new charges, but 'Andrew had the same naive experience – or lack of it – that we had,' chuckled Keith, 'He didn't know what was going on nor did we. We just learned as we went along.' [1]

Oldham appeared to model himself on 'Johnny Jackson', the fast-talking and irrepressibly confident Soho agent –who was, in turn, based on Larry Parnes, Britain's foremost pop impresario in the 1950s, and played by Laurence Harvey in 1959's quasi-satirical *Expresso Bongo* movie. The thrust of the plot was the metamorphosis of Bert Rudge – Cliff Richard's second big screen role – into a overnight Presley-esque figure via much browbeating hyperbole and media manipulation.

Unlike the fictitious Jackson, however, Oldham needed to share responsibility. 'He was in partnership with another guy,' elucidated Keith, 'and they were looking particularly for a new act to sign up for records and personal appearances. When you've been working backwater clubs for a year... well, in those days, a recording contract was almost as remote as God talking to you. Andrew was even younger than we were. He had nobody on his books, but he was a fantastic hustler. Although he didn't have much to offer, he did get people interested in what he was doing.' [7]

As mild-mannered as Oldham wasn't, Eric Easton, a former cinema organist, was married with children, and a self-confessed 'square'. [8] The depths of depravity for him were 20 filter-tips a day. Nevertheless, he knew showbusiness backwards, but, given to shaking a head to signify his wisdom, was quite content to let young Andrew be the Aaron to his Moses.

As Larry Parnes would have advised him, Easton saw his first task as transforming The Rolling Stones into altogether smoother pop entertainers. For a start – and with Oldham's consent – he compelled them to wear the uniform costumes he'd bought them for *Thank Your Lucky Stars*. When Keith followed Charlie's lead in loosening his matching slim-jim tie, he was ticked off – as Watts was for setting a bad example. Punctuality and back-projection were all-important too, but the group and Andrew were less convinced by Eric's arguments for playing to a fixed programme in the clubs and one-nighters that were still the Stones' bread-and-butter.

These engagements were becoming ticklish operations now, with outbreaks of screaming and even individual invasions of the stage from a majority of iron-bladdered girls who'd arrived ridiculously early in the front row to better gawk at Mick and Brian. Queues formed round the block, especially as dates in familiar haunts were becoming less and less frequent. 'I asked Keith once when he first knew that they were going to be big,' recalled Art Wood, leader of West London's jazzy Artwoods, 'and he said, "The audience told us – because every week, it was getting bigger and bigger". Once, Jagger rang me at Knighton Studios to ask if I could do Studio 51 one Sunday afternoon for 50 per cent of the door – because the Stones were *filming*. It was probably just a photo shoot, but that's when I realised that they'd made it – or were about to make it, even though they had too much of a rough edge to be a proper pop group in those days.'

It wasn't rough enough for Decca to turn its nose up at the Stones as the firm had the equally capable Beatles the previous year because there were sufficient guitar groups under contract already, thank you. All the same, best wishes for future success and blah blah blah, Mr Epstein. Thus wrote Dick Rowe, who'd been recognised as Decca's chief producer and talent spotter since his 'Broken Wings' by The Stargazers had been, in 1953, the first British disc to top the national chart. Later 1950s singers who also thrived under his aegis included Lita Roza, Dickie

Valentine and Billy Fury. Nonetheless, with Roza and Valentine in cabaret obsolescence; Fury on the wane and both The Beatles and Gerry And The Pacemakers poised to score another Number One each for EMI, Rowe's superiors weren't so sure about him anymore.

Desperate to climb back on his perch, he was ready to grant Eric Easton and this Oldham character more executive freedom than perhaps he should. 'I explained to Eric that I didn't want a standard record deal for them,' said Andrew. 'My strategy was based on what I had learned from Bob Crewe. He had signed The Four Seasons direct to VeeJay Records in the USA, and they made hits but never got paid. So they went to Philips and did a tape lease deal. This meant they made the records and delivered them. Philips just marketed them.'[9]

Maintaining quality control on output and ensuring that as few middlemen as possible were entitled to a cut, Oldham represented a new breed of learner-managers who viewed their clients as a longer-term prospect than commodities to be bought, sold and replaced when worn out. No matter how long their luck held, even Epstein and his Beatles expected it to run out at any second. 'It's been fun, but it won't last,' persisted John Lennon in 1964.[10]

'There was no precedent at that time,' added Keith Richards, 'You shot up there, and you were gone. There was no possible way you could believe that it was going to last for anything more than another two years. So for us, it was, like, the beginning of the end.'[11]

The threshold of despairing eminence coincided with the first hints of the erosion of Richards' friendship with Jones. 'We found out that he'd persuaded the powers that be that he ought to be taking five quid a week extra,' grimaced Keith. 'He used to get in all sorts of trouble and expect you to get him out of it. Everybody went through periods of trying to get along with him, but you're working and travelling every day, and you just don't have time to take care of this...fragile monster.'[1] Bill Wyman was to recall a specific incident 'when Keith gave Brian a black eye when he ate Keith's meat pie or something'.[12]

Keith's and Brian's subsequent history would be punctuated with unresolvable feuds, whispered onstage spite, *ménages à trois* and interminable petulance over seeming trifles. Jones forgetting to sing one of the 'That's what I want' antiphonies in 'Money' would become an issue all the more major through he and Richards being shoulder-to-shoulder for hours on end with the road roaring in everyone's ears when first the Stones ventured onto the ballroom circuit after 'Come On' was unleashed on 7 June 1963.

Motoring from Camberley's Agincourt to the Rock Garden in Llandrindod Wells to some Plaza or other in a town six counties to the northeast, they lay themselves open to incomprehension and derision from the mob shuffling about in front of them, now that Eric Easton's *Thank Your Lucky Stars* costumes had been abandoned along with his directives about 'wonderful-to-be-here' vapourings and performing what could be described, with a little logical blindness, as a smash hit. 'When we released our first single, we were doing gigs every night, and we refused to play it,' snarled Keith, 'How could we go out and do our set of heavy rhythm-and-blues, and then play this little pop song? It was too embarrassing.'[1]

Wantonly pleasing yourself rather than the audience could kindle extreme reaction from the many Teddy Boys that had remained at large despite the slings and arrows of fashion. Their displeasure at these long-haired ponces could be most painfully expressed in a shower of pre-decimalisation pennies cascading stagewards, carrying on after the lacerated visitors evacuated the boards, and throughout the master of ceremonies' attempts to restore order.

Yet under the stage lights, the Stones certainly looked and sounded Big Time – and, though he'd never admit it, a provincial

Ted couldn't really fault the musicianship or the Stones launching into unashamed classic rock from the 1950s if they felt like it. He'd read in the music press that negotiations for a support spot to Jerry Lee Lewis were under way. Nonetheless, the group's first countrywide tour would be with Bo Diddley, The Everly Brothers – and, at the eleventh hour, an exquisite who had exchanged the billowing drapes and overhanging pompadour he'd sported in *The Girl Can't Help It* for sober attire and a bristled scalp. Nothing, however, could belittle him in Keith's eyes: 'the most exciting moment of my life was appearing on the same stage as Little Richard'.[13]

The trek finished close to home at the Odeon in Rochester on 1 November – the day that 'I Wanna Be Your Man' was released. The Stones' implied association with The Beatles was a double-edged sword, now that 'the Fab Four' were a hit with grown-ups as well as teenagers. After they all but stole the Royal Variety Performance three days later, the general feeling among adults, and others who hadn't wanted to like them, was that John, George, Paul and Ringo were the stock Nice Lads When You Get To Know Them. Ireland's Bachelors – more Brook Brothers than Beatles – were even nicer lads who, as token pop group in the following autumn's Royal show, had been quite amenable to turning to face the Queen in her balcony for an amended opening titular line – '*we* wouldn't change *you* for the wurrrrld!' – of their most recent Top Ten strike.

If The Bachelors and The Beatles put themselves in the way of potentially damaging publicity – like one married Bachelor's *amour* with a well-known female vocalist or a Liverpool woman's imputation of her baby's irregular kinship to Paul McCartney – their respective investors would ensure that no nicotine-stained fingers would type out lurid coverage of it for the following Sunday's *News Of The World*. Besides, even if it was true, nothing too sordid was likely to be yet brought to public notice about The Beatles, The Bachelors, Gerry, Billy J

Kramer, The Fourmost and other ostensibly wholesome pop stars by a scum press who judged any besmirching of cheeky but innocent personas as untimely. Let's save the scandal for The Rolling Stones, to be cited by one tabloid – who set all the others off – as 'the ugliest group in Britain',[14] following their languid and offhand judgement on the latest singles – voting every one of them a 'miss' – on BBC television's *Juke Box Jury* on 27 June 1964.

No edition of the show has ever been as controversial but, long before that, Eric Easton had recognised that he had failed miserably to make the Stones as clean-cut and as amiable as The Bachelors and The Beatles. Once upon a time, they'd toed a winsome line, what with Keith *Richard* stating in the first fan club biography that his ambition was to appear at the London Palladium, the very pinnacle of conventional British showbusiness. He'd also given his former profession as 'post office worker'.[15] Now he was saying he'd been a 'layabout', compounding this infamy by listing 'policemen' among his 'hates' in the *New Musical Express*'s 'Lifelines' tabulation.[16] To no avail, too, Eric had stressed the importance of making themselves pleasant to reporters and fans. If a stranger came up to *Richard* and said, 'Hello Keith. How is your brother Cliff?', Eric – and Decca – would rather a polite lie along the lines of, 'Fine, thanks. He's keeping well' than Keith asking the enquirers why he didn't bugger off.

Finally, Easton gave up, deciding instead to place that side of things on the more with-it shoulders of Andrew Loog Oldham, who, noticed Keith Richards, 'always made sure we were as violent and as nasty as possible'.[12]

5 The Anti-Beatle

'The way they arranged "Not Fade Away" was the
beginning of the shaping of them as songwriters.'
— *Andrew Loog Oldham*[1]

As anti-Beatles, the Stones cut appositely baleful figures on the
front photograph of an eponymous debut long-player – though
anyone awaiting seething musical outrage was disappointed
because its content didn't ring many changes as it was as weighty
with R&B standards as each of the debut albums yet to come by
The Animals, The Yardbirds, The Kinks, The Downliners Sect,
Them, The Pretty Things and The Spencer Davis Group – and
the first two Beatles LPs put together.

However, unlike *Please Please Me*, if not *With The Beatles*,
The Rolling Stones didn't include any of their chart entries. On
future 'best of' and 'greatest hits' collections, 'Come On' would
be selected for its historical importance if nothing else, but 'I
Wanna Be Your Man' tended to be omitted. Neither did Keith
list 'Lennon-McCartney' among 'favourite composers' in
'Lifelines'. Nevertheless, intrigued when John and Paul had
completed 'I Wanna Be Your Man' virtually to order when
looking in at a Stones rehearsal in 1963, Richards and Jagger
took their first uncertain steps as a songwriting duo.

'We weren't going to give them anything great, were we?' was
Lennon's rhetorical confession in one of his last interviews.[2] Had
they done so, Brian Epstein may have felt that they were giving
too much of a leg up to potentially dangerous competitors. This

was justifiable on the evidence of the *NME* readers' popularity poll for 1963, which placed the Stones behind The Springfields, The Shadows, Gerry And The Pacemakers, The Searchers and The Beatles, but ahead of Freddie And The Dreamers, Brian Poole And The Tremeloes – and even The Hollies, the biggest fish to be hooked in Manchester after Liverpool had been left to rot as, like pillaging Vikings of old, the contract-waving host from London had swept eastwards.

A couple of Hollies had been present for the session for 'Not Fade Away', a 1957 Crickets B-side, reworked by Keith on acoustic guitar to sound more like that summer's posthumous Buddy Holly solo hit, a vibrant revival of 'Bo Diddley' that retained the self-dedicating Bo's signature shave-and-a-haircut-six-pence rhythm. 'Andrew has often been quoted as saying that, so far as he was concerned, Keith had written the song,'[3] sniggered Tony Calder, with whom Oldham was to form a business partnership while the one with Eric Easton soured.

Though Keith had told the *NME* that he was saving up for a houseboat on the Thames, he, Andrew and Mick were now living on the second floor of 33 Mapesbury Road that, if in a rather shabby 1930s terrace in West Hampstead's bedsitter land (and, incidentally, close to Decca's main studio complex), was palatial compared to 102 Edith Grove. According to Richards, it was here that Oldham 'just locked us in a kitchen for a day, and said, "When you come out, make sure you come out with a song". To me – and to Mick – writing a song was as different as someone who makes a saddle for a horse, and someone who puts the shoes on [but] it gives you the confidence to think, well, if we can write one, we can write two.'[3]

They had the unmitigated audacity to send a tape of a ditty entitled 'Give Me Your Hand' – which wasn't 'anything great' either – to The Beatles. Among other of their first stockpiled efforts, 'Tell Me', stuck out like a sore thumb on the debut LP because it had more to do with Bobbies Vee, Vinton and Rydell than Muddy Waters, Bo Diddley or Chuck Berry. Possibly for this very reason, demonstration tapes of more of the same were submitted and accepted by would-be pop stars grubbing around London's music-publishing offices. The otherwise unsung George Bean And The Runners' second 45, for instance, was Richards and Jagger's repetitive 'It Should Be You', while Bobby Jameson, a Paul McCartney lookalike but fair-headed, tried 'Each And Every Day Of The Year' (with Keith credited as 'musical director'). Then there'd be 'So Much In Love',[4] 'Blue Turns To Grey' and '(Walkin' Thru' The) Sleepy City', successive A-sides by Rugby's Mighty Avengers and 'I'd Much Rather Be With The Boys' – attributed to Richards and Oldham – by The Toggery Five, runners-up to The Bo Street Runners in a national talent contest organised by ITV's *Ready Steady Go!*, an innovative pop series that prospered on interaction between performers and audiences.

Though The Mighty Avengers' 'So Much In Love' was to snatch slight chart honours, monetary rewards for Keith and Mick as composers were meagre until another number given the George Bean treatment, 'My Only Girl', was revamped as 'That Girl Belongs To Yesterday' by Gene Pitney, a US balladeer. Bar the remote Elvis, he – with Roy Orbison and, though hits were thin on the ground after 1961, Jerry Lee Lewis – came to command the most devoted UK following for a foreign artiste during a lean time for North American pop. He merited such respect for an understated stage persona if not his distinctive nasal tenor. The lesser follow-up to his famous 'Twenty-Four Hours From Tulsa', 'That Girl Belongs To Yesterday' chased 'Not Fade Away' into the British Top Ten, and even sneaked into the US *Hot 100*, affording the songwriting Stones some quiet pride.

Penned to order, their 'As Tears Go By' roamed the domestic Top 20 when sung by Marianne Faithfull, a blonde 17-year-old from Berkshire in whom Andrew Loog Oldham had seen pop star potential, and for whom Jagger entertained romantic designs. Though it was to resurface as a Stones B-side late in 1965, Keith considered it then 'the sort of song we'd never play. We were trying to write "Hoochie Coochie Man", and came out with a song that's almost like "Greensleeves".'³

For Marianne, this breakthrough was dampened by the failure of her second 45, 'Blowin' In The Wind', an anti-war opus from *The Freewheelin' Bob Dylan*, and a hit previously by Peter, Paul and Mary, also from New York's bohemian Greenwich Village. Keith developed quite a fondness for Dylan, who was about to upset folk pedants by 'going electric' and exposing rock 'n' roll influences. 'Obviously Five Believers' on his *Blonde On Blonde Meisterwerk*, for instance, would seem to be inspired by 'I Want To Be Your Driver' from 1965's *Chuck Berry In London*.⁵

As well as being delighted to finger-pick guitar on Faithfull's 'Blowin' In The Wind', Keith's moptop-gone-to-seed was often covered with a peaked cap like Bob's when he was seen squiring Linda Keith, a photographic model and 'wild child' daughter of a Light Programme presenter, around late-night London watering holes. Linda was 20-year-old Keith's first 'serious' girlfriend. The peaks and troughs of their two-year entanglement would embrace his disapproval of her alleged frolicking with heroin, a summer holiday in the south of France and him looking through the eyes of love when facial scars of a car crash in which she was involved were still raw.

Little privacy had been very much the way of things at Edith Grove, and even at Mapesbury Road there'd nearly always be someone else hovering should a tenant and his paramour choose to canoodle on the living-room settee. However, after Andrew married in September 1964, only Mick would be party to any of Linda and Keith's sweet nothings when he and Richards moved to a chalet-style apartment with an extended lounge and fitted wardrobes on the edge of Hampstead Heath, the most verdant part of North London. It was also sufficiently up-market to

KEITH RICHARDS

attract burglars – who turned the place over when the Stones were on their fourth national tour in almost as many months.

This latest trip was in the wake of the first of five consecutive Number Ones, a cover of 'It's All Over Now' by The Valentinos – a US chart entry so minor that it didn't warrant a release in Europe. The Stones' standing in market terms was reflected too in the high-pitched adulation and general consternation that spread wherever they passed – or were about to pass. At each proposed stop, hundreds ringed themselves days in advance around theatres, cinemas and city halls to guarantee admission. Those lacking such clubbable stamina recoursed to buying tickets from touts at up to eight times the marked price.

At Plymouth, it was necessary to smuggle the Stones along underground tunnels leading from Westward Television's studios two blocks away to a lane beside the ABC. At a given signal, a fire exit was flung open and the group was striding purposefully and unobserved along the passageway towards it when a female let out a shriek and brought an adoring mob down on them.

Not everyone was so besotted with them. Posses of short-maned males, maddened by the Stones' now shoulder-length tresses, would arm themselves with scissors and plan depilatory barbarity on the five nancy-boys who'd taken the mick by placing an ad in a December edition of the *NME* wishing starving hairdressers and their families a Happy Christmas. No such aggressor got past the stage door but, had he succeeded, he may have been repulsed by what Keith had learned from a dabbling with karate with Andrew – or, more insidiously, his ability to outface unwanted company in the dressing rooms where he and the others would be incarcerated until, with the cadence of the last song still reverberating, they bolted pell-mell to a getaway car ticking over in a back alley.

A police cordon with helmets rolling in the gutter held back clamorous fans who chased the vehicle up the high street. 'Basically, we'd turn up, and all we'd think about is, "What's the exit strategy?",' explained Keith, 'and then we'd take bets on how many songs we'd get through before it all collapsed. Usually, it was ten minutes – three songs and it was all over. We'd walk into some of those places, and it was like they had the Battle of the Crimea [*sic*] going on. "Scream power" was the thing everyone was judged by. We couldn't hear ourselves for years.'[6]

During one 1964 month, The Beatles were traversing the country at the same time, and it might be instructive to compare the behaviour of their public then with that of the Stones. Police patrolled the all-night queues that had formed before box offices opened, but no bother was expected from the occupants of the sleeping bags that lined the pavements with their transistor radios and comics. Once they might have wrung their hands, but now mums and dads would bring provisions to their waiting children. Well, it was only The Beatles, ritualised and cosy.

In the auditorium, the girls let rip their healthy, good-humoured screams. Sure, there was fainting and heightened blood pressure brought on nosebleeds. The odd tip-up chair would snap off its spindle too, but after 'Twist And Shout', the screeching would cease for the National Anthem, resuming half-heartedly before the audience filed out quietly.

Only fire hoses could quell riots at shows by those sinister Rolling Stones, however. A judgement on them was that among the 22 unconscious after one such fiasco – the first house at Manchester's Odeon on 3 October 1965 – lay Keith Richards, stunned by a flying lemonade bottle. On the sodden carpeting, auditorium cleaners would come across soiled knickers among smashed rows of seating.

If teenagers had to like beat groups, reasoned grown-up Britain, let it be ones like The Beatles, Herman's Hermits or The Dave Clark Five, more palatable than these Rolling Stones or their blood brothers, The Pretty Things, whose similarly abandoned performances and reprobate image had held instant appeal for record companies looking for an act to combat

Decca's Stones coup. A 1964 single, 'Rosalyn', had irritated the Top 30, paving the way for the Things' biggest smash, 'Don't Bring Me Down'. Next, a Dick Taylor original, 'Honey I Need', clambered almost as high early in 1965 when the Things and the Stones were still on terms of fluctuating commercial equality. Then paths diverged; the Stones suffering international acclaim and supertax while the Things began over 30 years of struggle and heartache that might have destroyed a lesser group.

Yet it was the Things rather than the Stones who were seen as the patron saints of the also-rans typified by The Mustangs, who took what the *Herald Of Wales* described as a 'big gamble'[7] by replacing all their Top 20 pop with R&B. No longer milking their audiences either, Stan Webb's Shades Five became Chicken Shack by 1965, and Tony And The Talons from nearby Warwick mutated into The Original Roadrunners. 'There were two factions in the band,' recollected frontman Edgar Broughton, 'One for the rural country stuff, and one for the Chicago-type blues.'[8]

Yet, when scrimmaging around the dim-lit and often insalubrious clubs that were now littering British towns – Tuesday nights in Andover's Copper Kettle, say, or Bluesville in a Sheffield pub, the Gamp in Edinburgh or Rhythm Unlimited beneath the shadow of Birmingham Town Hall – long-haired R&B outfits were discovering that, while 'Hoochie Coochie Man', 'I Got My Mojo Working', John Lee Hooker's leering 'Dimples' and so forth went down a storm onstage, on vinyl, their blunt lyrics and stylised chord cycles did not merit inclusion even in a 1964 Top 50 that had welcomed Howlin' Wolf's repromoted 'Smokestack Lightning' and The Yardbirds' 'surfing' arrangement of Sonny Boy Williamson's 'Good Morning Little Schoolgirl'. Craving for the hit that might lift them off the club treadmill too, The Hullaballoos would peroxide hair splayed halfway down their backs, while The Primitives had theirs trimmed to short-back-and-sides on a TV chat show in an ill-judged publicity stunt.

Men don't have periods and can't get pregnant, but pillars of Women's Liberation might note how difficult the issue of hair could be for boys when even the coolest parents battled for control of their features when the Stones or Pretty Things were on *Top Of The Pops*. 'It seems so ridiculous now,' chuckled Phil May, once the wearer of the longest male hair in mid-1960s Britain, 'There was trouble in the streets all the time. If I walked down Erith High Street, people would jeer and try to pick a fight. Even at art school, we used to go around in pairs.'

On the road, the Things endured last-minute cancellations by hoteliers, punch-ups with parochial hobbledehoys and, in one cultural backwater, some unpleasantness with a shotgun. Dick Taylor would recount, 'After the gig, we walked out of the place, and some guy made a remark about Phil's hair, and I said something back. Then these rather heavy-looking yokels – like a lynch mob – started pursuing us, and Philip "the Greek" Andropolis, our minder-cum-driver, suddenly produced these coshes and other weapons from the car and stuck them in our hands. Next, he got the shotgun out. Instead of backing off, this guy got totally enraged and grabbed the end of it. Philip started swinging him around. Passers-by sort of ignored it. Perhaps it was a normal Saturday night in Swindon – but, fortunately, a policeman arrived. In the end, Philip was done for not having a firearms licence.'

Elsewhere in the sticks, however, the locals were like friendly, if over-attentive, wolfhounds. 'We'd turn up at places where there'd be two or three thousand people in the car park,' expounded Phil May, 'At the Giaconda, a coffee bar in Hull, we couldn't get near the place until the organisers arranged for us and our equipment to be passed over the heads of the crowd and manhandled onto this tiny stage.'

The Stones were above one-nighters by the middle of 1964 but over the years they'd punctuate tours with roots-affirming dates in venues of comparable size to the 200-capacity

Giaconda. Among the first of these was Studio 51. On its walls in 1964 were full-size blow-ups of both the departed Stones and The Downliners Sect, a Middlesex quintet holding sway there for much of that year. They could boast The Kinks among their support acts, shortly before the latter began a six-year chart run.

'Just after a Sunday afternoon spot, Mick and Keith – who were a bit of a double act – walked into Studio 51,' detailed bass guitarist Keith Grant. 'They asked if they could appear with us as they missed the atmosphere of the small clubs – so we picked a date when they were free to do so. However, on the night, after they'd done a couple of songs, someone pulled the plug on them – possibly because they were upset that the Stones had "deserted" the place by becoming famous. The plug was put back in, but was pulled out again after a few more numbers – so I stationed myself by the plug to stop it happening again.'

Another uproarious reunion took place in 1965 when, following a truncated set on 7 March 1965 at the Palace Theatre in Manchester – where a girl was injured, falling from the dress circle – Keith and Mick taxied across the city to leap onstage for a few numbers with The Pretty Things, who happened to be appearing at the Manchester Cavern that same evening. Such *esprit de corps* also extended to an Artwoods booking at a new London venue, Blaises, which was dignified by the presence in the audience of Richards and Brian Jones, who invited Art Wood to their table during the interval 'where we chatted just like old mates – which we were,' said Art.

United by artistic purpose and mutual respect, easy offstage camaraderie had resulted too in Keith's show of kindness in championing The Flintstones, a horn-laden combo on the Little Richard tour, as his 'favourite band' in 'Lifelines'. He also sought the particular company of Alan Taylor, guitarist with Dave Berry's Cruisers, when the two groups' paths crossed in roadside café or backstage corridor, as well as that of Veronica 'Ronnie' Spector of US vocal group The Ronettes, who co-headlined a round-Britain expedition with the Stones in January 1964. She found Richards 'not so much shy as quiet. I could make him laugh, but most of the time, nothing was funny to him. He was very much himself in his own room and his own world.'[9]

6 The Fuzz Boxer

'You had to be the biggest dreamer in the world to think you could export this stuff to America.'

– Keith Richards [1]

Weeks prior to The Beatles' messianic descent on Kennedy Airport, the 'British Invasion' of North America had been an eventuality predicted by Gene Pitney when he'd touched down in New York in late 1963 with the screams from a slot on *Thank Your Lucky Stars* – with The Rolling Stones on the bill too – still ringing in his ears. Within a year, all manner of US showbiz personalities would be paying artist-to-artist respects to incoming British pop celebrities, among them Elvis, who'd welcome Herman's Hermits to his Beverley Hills mansion; Zsa Zsa Gabor, who'd have her picture taken with George Harrison; Frank Sinatra, shaking hands and chatting affably with Keith Richards and Andrew Oldham when they looked in at a session at Hollywood's Western Recording Studio.

After this sub-continent had capitulated, the rest of the world was a walkover. Once, your group had had as much chance of getting a record in the charts of even the local newspaper as the lead singer had of being knighted, but nowadays, if the van had drawn up outside a ballroom on Pluto, it might not have seemed all that peculiar. There you were, miming your latest hit on *Brisbane Tonight* or, like Frank Allen of The Searchers, touring New Zealand with the Stones: 'I stood watching them, mesmerised by the energy if not overawed by the expertise. A fan by my side remarked that Keith Richards could make his guitar talk. I could see what he meant – and I could almost hear the guitar saying, "Take your hands off me, you clumsy oaf," but it was impressive, of that there was no doubt. This was not so much a demonstration of music as a display of sex and power, and on that level, it worked to perfection.'[2]

Keith's riposte to Frank might have been, 'I've always done things on a fairly instinctive basis. I think brains have got in the way of too many things, especially something as basic as what we're doing.'[3]

Primitivism wasn't the way of The Searchers. Yet, while they'd wished they were in hell rather than Hamburg at first, it had been punishing seasons in that city's red-light district clubland that had toughened them up in readiness for what lay ahead. Similarly, a month's exploratory hard graft in the States in June 1964 was the Stones' 'Hamburg' in that it was often arduous but contained hidden blessings. Hitless there, the group was obliged to melt the *sang froid* of non-screaming curiosity seekers, and, though they were judged and found wanting on a couple of poorly attended occasions, other audiences – crucially, those at two performances at Carnegie Hall, New York's premier auditorium – felt a compulsion to dance only a few bars into the first number, and were, metaphorically, eating off the palm of Jagger's hand by the finish on the evidence of the bedlam that you could hear back in the dressing rooms.

The Stones had been determined not to quit the stage until the entire place was jumping, while making a run of the most frantic rockers all the more piquant by hanging fire midway and inserting doe-eyed 'Tell Me' – which, as a US A-side, would begin a slow ascent of the *Hot 100* by the time they flew back to London.

Nevertheless, while the likes of The Searchers, The Dave Clark Five, The Kinks and The Animals were ensconced in the Top Ten, the Stones were still struggling as US chart propositions when they undertook another jaunt before the year was out. This time, however, it was more like a re-run of British beat hysteria, what with a show at Lowe's Theatre, Providence, being stopped after four numbers, and the local group that opened proceedings, Georgie Porgie And His Fabulous Cry Babies, copying the Stones' repertoire, offhand stagecraft and appearance to the degree that chief show-off Porgie had been expelled from high school for hair length that exceeded the establishment's dress code. 'It wasn't long at all,' he protested, 'It would be considered less than average today.' Porgie's parents pursued the matter, taking it all the way to the US Supreme Court. 'It took them so long,' laughed Porgie, 'that everybody had long hair by then. There was no longer any point in hearing the case.'[4]

However, when the Stones ventured in 1964 to the heart of the Deep South 'Bible Belt', I Corinthians 11:14, 'Doth not nature itself teach you that if a man have long hair, it is a shame unto him?, was quoted by 'redneck' whites, who laced right-wing militancy with pious fear not so much of 'God' as of 'The Lord', a homespun prairie Plato with a crew cut, a Charles Atlas-like build and a hatred of commies, niggers – and queers like this new breed of 'musical' Limey longhairs.

A few snatched hours of serenity around a Savannah swimming pool were interrupted when, recounted Keith, 'we were arrested for topless bathing. Some people were driving by, and swore that there was a load of chicks leaping in and out of the pool with just a pair of drawers on. So the cops came zooming in to bust these "chicks" – and, of course, the closer they got, the more stupid they must have felt – especially when they heard these *sarf* London accents.'[5]

By then, half the dialects of Britain were resounding on US television and radio programmes aimed at teenagers. As well as Keith and Mick, northeast Kent was to be represented by Crispian St Peters – and, via filmed snippets, including an interview direct from Dick Taylor's parents' front room, The

Pretty Things. Allied with US radio censoring the line 'I laid her on the ground' from 'Don't Bring Me Down', and the issue of a 'decent' version by something called 'On Her Majesty's Service', North America was thus primed for a freak carnival of potentially greater magnitude than that centred on the Stones. Yet the moment was lost forever through the dithering of their management: big place, America, isn't it?

'Britain hasn't been so influential in American affairs since 1775,' cried a *Billboard* editorial[6] as fascination with all things pop to do with our sceptred isle were about to peak with two-thirds of the *Hot 100* British in origin. Though one record company executive was overheard cawing, 'I tell ya, Elmer, ya heard one Limey outfit, ya heard 'em all,' most of our major pop acts – and some minor ones – were staking claims in the commercial diggings. While they couldn't get arrested at home, The Hullaballoos' relentlessly opportunist US touring was paying off with *Hot 100* strikes. Less honourable attempts to crack the States at the expense of domestic success were made by Steve Marriott's Moments, who made a futile attempt to put one over on The Kinks by covering the latter's first domestic Number One, 'You Really Got Me', for the US only. Dave Berry's 'The Crying Game' was abducted likewise by Ian And The Zodiacs, who took it to Number One in Texas while sliding towards poverty-stricken disbandment back in their native Liverpool.

With most of the Union's 50 states comparable in size to the whole of Britain, it proved viable, too, for US labels with rights to Stones product to hurl at such a wide sales domain singles of any tracks from forthcoming or already big-selling LPs that took their fancy. Thus 'Time Is On My Side' intruded on the national Top 20 in summer 1964 – and 'Heart Of Stone' during the Christmas sell-in.

Less than two years later, the Stones would be arguably, if briefly, ahead of The Beatles in North America. Casting nervous backwards glances, the Merseysiders would snipe at the Stones in the press – hardly ever vice-versa – while sending an underling out mid-session to purchase their chief rivals' latest release. Nevertheless, both groups socialised outside working hours. Richards and Jagger, for example, were among party guests after The Beatles' concert before a record-breaking 56,000 at Shea Stadium in August 1965, and were often sighted holding court with Lennon and McCartney in one or other of about ten fashionable London nighteries for which Top 20 *conquistadores* could select a night out – with 'night' defined as around midnight to dawn.

Like most progressive R&B aficionados, Keith's, John's, Mick's and Paul's respective record collections reflected an advanced awareness of the US 'soul music' that forever filled the discos' deafening dark at the Scotch of St James, the Speakeasy, Blaises, the Pickwick or wherever else was currently 'in'. Before saturation, plugging on Britain's new pirate radio stations put them either in the charts' lower rungs or onto record decks in provincial clubland. Richards had long been *au fait* with eruditions like 'Harlem Shuffle' by Bob and Earl, and Edwin Starr's 'Headline News', as well as the originals of such UK covers as The Hollies' 'Just One Look' (Doris Troy), The Spencer Davis Group's 'I Can't Stand It' (The Soul Sisters), The Untamed's 'I'll Go Crazy' (James Brown), Carl Wayne And The Vikings' 'My Girl' (Otis Redding)[7] and The Kinks' 'Dancing In The Street' (Martha And The Vandellas).

The same applied to black styles from the West Indies. Access to the raw material had been mainly via import shops in suburbs with a pronounced Caribbean immigrant population, and the ear being caught by 'turntable hits' at metropolitan hang-outs like the Roaring Twenties and the Crazy Elephant. Thus, amid the post-Merseybeat holocaust had been the infiltration of 'bluebeat' – derived from the ska-mento-calypso crucible – into the UK Top 50 in 1964. Soaring into the very Top Ten had been a revival of 'Mockin' Bird Hill' from the

1940s, invested with a hiccuping 'bluebeat' lope by Tottenham's Migil Five, and 'My Boy Lollipop', a worldwide smash by Jamaica's own Millie, whose pipsqueak vocal and engaging personality had fascinated Chris Blackwell, a well-to-do Anglo-Jamaican who became her manager. Related to Crosse and Blackwell – the soup people – his Irish father had married into the Lindos, prominent Jews who had fled to the Caribbean from the burnings of the Spanish Inquisition.

West Indian music – and, indirectly, Blackwell – weren't yet to leave a mark on Richards and Jagger's songwriting, which was now closing the gap on Lennon and McCartney's formidable headstart. As much as it was with The Beatles, Stones albums were being scoured for potential hits by other artists, who were also courting Keith and Mick for the many numbers they'd penned that were unsuitable for the group.

Yet while 'That Girl Belongs To Yesterday', 'As Tears Go By' and Cliff Richard's 'Blue Turns To Grey' – with the demo serving as a German flip-side for the Stones – were money-spinners, whither the likes of 'Blue Turns to Grey' by both The Epics and, from California, Dick and Dee Dee – not to mention Vashti's 'Some Things Just Stick In Your Mind', 'Wastin' Time' by comedian Jimmy Tarbuck or 'You Must Be The One' from The Greenbeats? Either they made deflated journeys onto the deletion rack or were buried on B-sides.

While these syndications were life's loose change in every sense of the phrase, Keith and Mick were flattered rather than insulted when Otis Redding had the gall to revive '(I Can't Get No) Satisfaction' as a Top 40 single within months of it being the first of many Rolling Stones *Hot 100* Number Ones. Yet, if Richards' and Jagger's most 'covered' opus too,[8] 'Satisfaction' was little liked by Keith to whom its defining *ostinato* occurred when he was jerked from sleep, bedevilled by an impulse to note it on the transistorised tape recorder that had become as essential as a toilet bag in his luggage.

Amused by the memory, he'd recreate how, 'The next morning, I listened to the tape, and there was about two minutes of an acoustic guitar playing a very rough riff, and then me snoring for forty'.[9] After the song had been launched into more tangible life, he worried about what appeared to be its stomach-knotting similarity to 'Dancing In The Street'. Another concern was that 'I can't get no satisfaction from the judge' had opened a verse of the litigational Chuck Berry's 'Thirty Days' from 1955.

Any infuriating familiarity wasn't as apparent to the other Stones when they assembled in May 1965 to tape 'Satisfaction', the 'Beethoven's Fifth' of 1960s pop, at Chicago's Leonard Chess Studio, venerated as the wellspring of classics by Muddy, Wolf, Diddley, Berry, you name 'em. 'We had a harmonica on it then,' said Richards, 'and it was considered to be a good B-side or maybe an LP track. A week later, we recorded it again in Los Angeles. This time, everything went right.'[10]

Nevertheless, part of the Otis Redding arrangement's appeal to Keith would be the horn section punching out the riff – as the resident band did on the final bars when the Stones premiered 'Satisfaction' on the US pop show *Shindig*. On the disc, an attempt to approximate this effect had been made with the aid of a device called a 'fuzzbox' attached to the 1959 Les Paul Standard – reputedly, the first in Britain – that Richards had brought back from the Stones' first US trip. When designed by Gibson in 1962, the Maestro Fuzztone had been intended to make a guitar sound like a saxophone but, through Keith, its blackboard-scratching hoarseness would assume a personality of its own.[11]

A contemporary of Georgie Porgie and another Providence combo of like persuasion, The Mojo Hands, Dennis Blackledge was to write, 'It was new. It was bold. It was trashy. "Satisfaction" captured in one song the essence of what The Mojo Hands aspired to be. They put it on their playlist the day after. They added a fuzz-box to their arsenal shortly after that.

'One theory has The Rolling Stones receiving their inspiration for the "Satisfaction" sound from watching The Standells play "Dirty Water" at clubs in and around the Los Angeles area. As luck would have it, "Satisfaction" was released first, and now everyone assumes The Standells lifted the "Dirty Water" sound from the Stones.'[4]

While Keith Richards may not have read Blackledge's disobliging remarks, Bob Dylan told him to his face that 'I could have written "Satisfaction", but you couldn't have written "Desolation Row".'[9] If nothing else, the latter, approaching the quarter-hour mark as the finale of 1965's *Highway 61 Revisited* 'released everyone from that whole three minute thing,' noted Keith, 'Not to mention making it unnecessary to use sentiments based around "I Want To Hold Your Hand".'[3]

He went on, 'Bob showed us all a new approach, new ways of writing songs. He came from a folk tradition, which had much looser possibilities, and he showed you that rock 'n' roll didn't have to be quite so restricted by that verse-chorus-verse formula. We all pushed each other in those days.'[5]

Like anybody who appreciated lyrical poetry, Richards understood that Dylan was jolting pop's under-used brain into reluctant action with his rapid-fire literariness, incongruous connections (such as 'Einstein disguised as Robin Hood' in 'Desolation Row') and streams of consciousness. Keith, however, wasn't then much of a wordsmith himself, preferring to focus on melody, riffs and chord structures. 'It's sound I'm after, not so much a piece of music,' he enlarged, 'Getting ideas for songs is a totally unconscious process.'[12]

The entourage had learned to leave him alone and field all outside interference whenever, as Marianne Faithfull observed, he'd 'take the germ of a song and nag at it, all the while keeping himself to himself. He played the guitar constantly. I never saw him without it.'[13]

'If you have a question about the lyric, ask Mick,' was Keith's reply to a question about a new Stones 45, 'That's his department.'[14] Yet, while Richards seemed to suggest that he attended to the music and Jagger, the words, the partnership was less cut-and-dried Rodgers and Hammerstein (or Lloyd-Webber and Rice) with defined demarcation lines than Lennon-McCartney whereby creative functions dissolved and merged, often under immense market pressures.

'Satisfaction' was still lingering in the *Hot 100* when 'Get Off Of My Cloud' was rush-released in October 1965. It was, opined Keith, 'one of Andrew's worst productions. Actually, what I wanted to do was slow it down, but we rocked it up'.[5] Mere weeks later, the group would be hustled into the same studios – RCA in Hollywood – for the first of two block-booked sessions of less than a few days each, from plug-in to final mix, for *Aftermath*, an LP that was a conscious musical progression from the previous patchworks of R&B-soul stand-bys and uneasy originals.

A year after their first British A-side ('The Last Time') for the group, Richards and Jagger – never that receptive to the compositions of colleagues – were sufficiently self-assured to write all 14 tracks on *Aftermath*, selected from detailed demo tapes to half-finished music with odds and ends of lyrics. While the engineer was occupied with some tedious mechanical process of spools, switches and faders, Jagger might be on the other side of the glass-fronted booth collating the rest of the verses as Richards teased a tune or chord sequence from his guitar – like painters dabbing at a hanging canvas minutes before the gallery opens. Yet, if The Beatles were now spending days on end on one track, any extension of *Aftermath*'s time limit might have detracted from the proceedings' spontaneity and endearing imperfections.

When the LP reached Number One in both the US and Britain – proving once again that sales figures for singles were but a surface manifestation of deeper devotion – it became clear that the Stones were as sound an investment for Decca as The Beatles were for EMI. The budget was, therefore, stretched to their requisitioning of orchestral strings to fairy-dust the 'As Tears Go By' that was coupled with '19th Nervous Breakdown', the A-side that followed 'Get Off Of My Cloud' – and, after Otis Redding-esque horns drove 'Got To Get You Into My Life' on The Beatles new album, *Revolver*, trumpets did likewise on 'Have You Seen Your Mother Baby Standing In The Shadow', albeit a single that, stalling at Number Five at home and Nine in the States, was a comedown by recently established standards.

If the result of multiple overdubs by Brian Jones rather than a phalanx of session shellbacks playing at the same time, what sounded like a colliery silver band tootled and rasped beneath 'Something Happened To Me Yesterday' on *Between The Buttons*, the album that marked time artistically after *Aftermath*. This number amounted to a Jagger–Richards duet. Soon, Keith alone, rather than Bill and Brian – or himself and Brian (as heard on the Beach Boys-esque 'baw-baw-baws' on *Aftermath*'s 'What To Do') – would be evident, where necessary, on harmonies that were integrations into the lead vocal rather than unison responses, indicating perhaps lessons learned from the small chorales of The Beatles, The Hollies, The Searchers, The Byrds – and now The Pretty Things via the enlistment of new personnel from the ranks of Bern Elliott's Fenmen.

Keith's baritone was louder than Mick's on *Between The Buttons*'s 'Connection', an opus that seems to contain references to the non-prescription drugs that helped the time pass quicker in this bandroom or on that long-haul flight. If all too aware of 'Purple Hearts', 'Black Bombers' and like pep pills, marijuana ('pot') had been a bit too cloak and dagger for most 1960s pop stars until no less than The Beatles had giggled through the shooting of their second movie, *Help!*, in the haze of its short-lived magic. Pot then came to be used more and more as a herbal handmaiden to creativity as certain groups started thinking of themselves as not just mere entertainers, but pseudo-mystics whose songs required repeated listening to comprehend what might be veiled but oracular messages. Even the bucolic Troggs were singing about 'the bamboo butterflies of yer mind', and were to suffer airplay restrictions for 1967's 'Night Of The Long Grass' on the ridiculous premise that it referred to drugs ('grass').

''67 was the explosion of the drug culture, if there is such a thing,' explained Keith. 'It came out into the open from underground, and everybody started talking about it.'[3] When not yet versed in hip jargon, the universal aunt that was the BBC had passed Bob Dylan's 'Rainy Day Women Nos. 12 & 35' (with its 'Everybody must get stoned!' hook-line), but just plain 'Heroin' by The Velvet Underground and 'The Addicted Man' by The Game[15] hadn't a hope of a single Light Programme (soon to be Radio One) spin. The Corporation had also frowned on The Byrds' 'Eight Miles High' and *Revolver*'s eerie omega 'Tomorrow Never Knows' as the 'us and them' divide between youth and elders over the issue of drugs intensified. It would climax halfway through 1967 – with Keith Richards on the very top of the midsummer bonfire.

7 Prisoner No. 7855

'Keith sort of sneered at anybody who tried to get too close. Mick's girlfriend, Chrissie Shrimpton, was a secretary type – Miss Proper, hairdresser's on Thursdays – and so was the girl Keith had: very plain, no challenge.'

– *Anita Pallenberg*[1]

After a Top Ten strike with The McCoys' 'Hang On Sloopy' had fanfared the founding of Immediate, Britain's first truly successful independent record label, in 1965 by Tony Calder and Andrew Oldham, Keith and Mick were employed as in-house composers and general factotums. Commercially, their clients ranged from duds like Twice As Much and Nicky Scott to chart-topping Chris Farlowe, produced by Jagger – as 1966's *Today's Pop Symphony* by The Aranbee Pop Symphony Orchestra was, apparently, by Keith.

Open to question, however, is the degree of Keith's involvement in this easy-listening *mélange* of current hits by The Beatles, Sonny and Cher, The Four Seasons, The Moody Blues and Wilson Pickett plus a generous helping of Jagger–Richards compositions.[2] If barely able to sight-read, he may have dah-dah-dahed the required scoring, but, although the concept of a Rolling Stones without Richards was unthinkable, the sub-text of the exercise may have been Oldham's endeavour to heighten the profile of one who was generally less popular with fans than Mick, Brian and Bill in surveys conducted by *Mirabelle*, *Jackie* and other schoolgirl comics. Moreover, while he was, in 1965, rated fourth in *Beat Instrumental*'s annual readers' poll for best lead guitarist – after The Shadows' Hank Marvin, Jeff Beck of The Yardbirds and George Harrison but in front of Eric Clapton, Jimmy Page, The Who's Pete Townshend[3] and Dave Davies of The Kinks – Richards had dropped to sixth the following year, overtaken by Clapton and The Spencer Davis Group's Steve Winwood.

In the rhythm guitarist section, Brian Jones, though of much as a lead player as Keith, held firm at fourth but, in hard financial terms, he swallowed dust behind Richards who, as well as his share of net income from concerts, was reaping such a harvest from his songwriting that, before he had so much as booked a driving lesson, there had been much bowing and scraping in a London car showroom as Keith had paced up and down rows of gleaming Bentleys fitted with all the latest electronically operated gadgetry. A week later, a blue Continental model was delivered, delayed by the adjustment of driving-seat contours to Keith's – not his chauffeur's – measurements.

From the same source, Doris Richards received an Austin 1100 from her son, for whom city lights had lost much of their allure, especially since giggling fans had winkled out the ex-directory number at the St John's Wood pied-à-terre he'd found after he and Mick had left Mapesbury Road, following neighbours' complaints about fans congregating outside. Since April 1966, therefore, Keith's principal residence had been far beyond the capital's outer conurbations.

Now as synonymous with his name as the Queen's with Windsor Castle, 'Redlands' was a spacious Tudor farmhouse with a thatched roof, a moat and foundations dating from the Norman Conquest. The odd poacher and hiker were the only intruders, and expected visitors would sometimes miss the tree-lined driveway along the main road that descended to the village of West Wittering and the Sussex yachting fraternity's sheltered harbour.

Brian Jones, still living within the drone of London traffic, may have envied Richards' isolation, where the only noise to disturb the stillness was the odd chivvying pheasant bursting from the woods. However, Keith was unashamedly impressed by Brian's new jet-setter girlfriend with her willowy figure and Marlene Dietrich-esque drawl, just the sort of 'chick' he would have liked for himself, especially as his affair with Linda Keith was fizzling out, and would be extinguished altogether after she, supposedly, cuckolded him with Jimi Hendrix.

Richards was to serve Jones likewise with Anita Pallenberg, born in Italy of mingled Swiss, German and Scandinavian stock. Her father, a 'frustrated composer',[4] ran a travel agency in Rome where his two daughters attended a German school. Gaining a consequent scholarship in graphic design, multilingual Anita accompanied painter boyfriend Mario Schifano to New York where beatnik bards Allen Ginsberg and Gregory Corso were among her social conquests – as was multimedia pop artist Andy Warhol.

The late Andy had brought humour and topicality back into art through his self-conscious fascination with junk aesthetics, which included pop music as much as his soup cans, Brillo pads and comic-strip philosophy. Stimulated by the celebrity of others, he'd been sneaked into the backstage area of a Manhattan theatre because, as he put it, 'I wanted to be in the presence of The Yardbirds.'[5] The Stones had warranted some fuss too when they visited Warhol's Studio 54 in downtown New York, where, sniggered Keith, 'they ruined a perfectly good theatre by filling it with faggots in boxing shorts, waving champagne bottles in front of your face'.[6] Studio 54 also spawned The Velvet Underground, whose leader, Lou Reed, would produce an onstage syringe to simulate the process of mainlining during 'Heroin' – a substance he would later say he'd never touched. The observations of others repudiated this claim.

Pallenberg hadn't had much to do with heroin – or, indeed, any hard drugs – when she returned to Europe six months later to be employed variously as a disinclined model ('too beautiful to get out of bed', according to her agent[7]), a photography studio assistant and a movie actress, initially with a walk-on in Fellini's symbolism-ridden satire *La Dolce Vita*. While on an assignment for *Vogue* magazine in Paris, she attracted more than a second glance from Volker Schlondorff, usually based in Munich as an up-and-coming director in the revitalisation of European art-house film-making. 'I stayed at his flat,' recounted Anita, 'and had a crash course in cinema – but even though I was in the middle of the New Wave, as it were, I was getting into rock 'n' roll.'[7]

Following her *entrée* into the Stones' coterie at a backstage soirée in Munich late in 1965, Anita had had ample opportunity to log the characteristics of the two members whose songwriting alliance was one of many founts of profound emotional confusion for Brian, her new beau. She felt most comfortable with the selectively amiable Keith who was 'in many ways, the man Mick wanted to be. Free and easy in his own skin, not uptight like Mick. He was tough when he had to be, never backed down, had a good time, really enjoyed drinking, drugs and carousing, enjoyed sex. Mick envied Keith and was jealous of me.'[1] She gathered too that, on the strength of a recent one-night stand with him, Marianne Faithfull had concluded that Richards might be the sex stud of the century, and that, in the Stones' hierarchy, 'Whoever allied himself with Keith would have the power.'[8]

When in London, Richards was omnipresent at the Chelsea apartment Pallenberg shared with Jones, and went along for the ride when Brian flew to Munich to watch Anita filming. With Mick and Marianne, he tagged along too when John Michell, author of 1967's *The Flying Saucer Mystery* and 1969's *View Over Atlantis*, indulged Brian's and Anita's interest in supersensory matters by conducting them to Woodhope Church, Hertfordshire, to investigate magnetic disturbances in ley lines. There was also a small-hours outing to Primrose Hill in the Bentley Continental to peer vainly in the city sky for extraterrestrials of the kind Keith professed to have seen in the gardens at Redlands.

As an overnight guest in Chelsea, Richards was sometimes privy to Jones' and Pallenberg's alternate bouts of wounding home truths and abrupt reconciliations. Noises from their bedroom would cover a waterfront from moans of ecstasy to bellowed trading of insults to outbursts of violence. 'Brian was very strong, and his assaults were terrible,' complained Anita, 'For days afterwards, I'd have lumps and bruises all over me.'[1]

Yet Keith couldn't help liking Brian Jones, despite the way he treated Anita (who, he noticed, was more inclined to retaliate than Brian's previous lovers), his childish malevolence on the road and the hypersensitivity that steered him into what appeared to others to be needless conflicts. Early in 1967, Jagger was Jones's principal *bête noire* when, 'Brian and I became firm friends again,' said Keith, 'I'd managed to break down a lot of barriers, but Brian always had to have an imaginary foe. He was a bit of a Don Quixote, I suppose. All I wanted to do was bring him into the mainstream again, but Brian used that to create a vendetta against Mick.'[9]

Brian was mistrustful of Andrew Loog Oldham too, but at least he – like Jagger – was a devil he knew. However, the gradual ousting of Eric Easton was well under way. Indeed, on 28 August 1965, Allen Klein had become the Stones' new co-manager. A hard-talking New Yorker, he was steeped in the complex mumbo-jumbo of US showbusiness lore, having learned much when assistant to Morty Craft, president of MGM in the late 1950s. Paunchy, short-cropped and an observer of a routine ruled by the clock, Klein had framed family photographs on his desk within the panelled top floor of a Manhattan skyscraper.

For all his methodically blunt stances on the telephone and in the board room, Allen was an impassive, reflective pipe-and-slippers sort at home who liked to distance himself from the office. He was everything Andrew Loog Oldham wasn't. Klein wouldn't be caught, for instance, nibbling afternoon scones at Redlands because he didn't 'bother that much with artists but you have to develop some sort of rapport – although it's important that you stay away. Otherwise you can really get on each other's nerves.'[10]

One of many Goldwyn-esque homilies ascribed to Klein was, 'What's the point of Utopia if it don't make a profit?' During 1967 – the so-called Age of Aquarius – it went without saying that Klein wasn't to succumb to kaftans, joss-sticks, meditation, Zen macrobiotic cookery or any other paraphernalia indicating a bedazzlement with the fake idealism of 'flower power'.

While Klein recognised that this fashionable travesty of love was just as much the latest transient craze as the Twist had been, he paid heed to its economic ramifications, chiefly that record companies were sinking more of their entrepreneurial acumen into albums rather than singles as pop – or, if you prefer, 'rock' – passed hastily through its 'classical' period. This was exemplified by The Pretty Things convincing fans that past *Top Of The Pops* excursions were now incidental to a main body of work on albums like their *SF Sorrow* 'rock opera', which they were thinking aloud of presenting as a ballet at Covent Garden. Eventually, it was staged as a musical play at the Roundhouse in Chalk Farm, with its backing tracks framing Phil May's narration and the other Things in acting roles. The story goes that the entire cast, and some of the audience, were under the influence of a trendy hallucinogenic called lysergic acid diethyalmide 25 – otherwise known as LSD.

George Harrison was to admit to taking it unknowingly when a mischievous dentist with whom he was friendly – 'a middle class swinger', reckoned John Lennon[11] – had concluded an otherwise pleasant evening by slipping into his guests' coffee a mickey finn of 'acid'. 'From the moment I had it,' confessed George, 'I wanted to have it all the time,' adding, 'It was important that people you were close to took it too.'[12]

Harrison and the other Beatles were talking openly about their psychedelic escapades, acknowledging no difference between the 'straight' press and underground journals like the fortnightly *International Times* – in which George, gaga with LSD, mentioned the 'magic eyes'[13] in the beads of his necklace, and a grasshopper that only he could see jumping into a speaker cabinet.

Keith Richards' initiation had pre-empted that of any Beatle. Until then, his illegal use of drugs hadn't gone beyond, say, some speed to wire him up for the show and a reefer to unwind tense coils within afterwards. Then he – and Brian – had been introduced to LSD by The Merry Band Of Pranksters, an itinerant troupe of performance artists (whose press releases promised, advisedly, 'a drugless psychedelic experience'). This took place hours after Keith had been knocked cold for several minutes by electric shock from an unearthed microphone on a stage in Sacramento on 4 December 1965.

Two years later, others who'd viewed the world from the Olympus of pop stardom since 1963 were also imbibing LSD as carelessly as alcohol. The Moody Blues and The Small Faces were among those who knew it well. 'Dropping acid' had become so commonplace in Swinging London that The Troggs were confined by their manager to provincial bookings to minimise the chances of heavy drug publicity sticking to them like it had to, say, Viv Prince, The Pretty Things' drummer — central figure of the first pop star drug bust – and The Rolling Stones after a more fabled event involving Richards and Jagger, triggered 'this incredible hassle,' gasped Keith, 'this sort of continual confrontation with policemen and judges. It did wear us down a bit'.[9]

Mick had been wary of LSD until he and Marianne Faithfull, now his 'constant companion', spent the weekend of 19 and 20 February 1967 at Redlands. Among the other guests were George Harrison and his wife, Pattie, an art dealer named Robert Fraser and a moneyed young Californian known as 'Acid King David', who was glad to breathe the groovy air round the Stones as an unpaid and unrecompensed minion.

David ingratiated himself with his host by producing tabs of 'Sunshine', a particularly refined type of LSD, for the party's use on an unusually mild Sunday morning – so mild that, after brunch, everyone climbed into a convoy of cars to search for a suitable starting point for a ramble round the surrounding countryside.

Back at Keith's by the early evening, the Harrisons decided to return to their home in Surrey. Their host maintains to this day that he'd have been immune from the trouble that followed if George of the Fab Four – England's darlings, now, with an MBE each – had stayed the night. In corroboration, an erroneous story went the rounds later that Harrison was still present, but was shooed away when, two hours later, the West Sussex Constabulary, armed with a search warrant, raided Redlands. Thanks to a tip-off from *The News Of The World*, then recipients of a libel writ from Jagger for alleging that he consumed controlled drugs, the force set to work to the sound, purportedly, of side one of Dylan's *Blonde On Blonde* – with provocative 'Rainy Day Women Numbers 12 and 35' the opening track – on automatic replay on Keith's stereo. They uncovered Marianne Faithfull clothed in nothing but a furry counterpane, following a bath; a quantity of cannabis (or 'Indian hemp' as it read on the report) about Acid King David's person; some tablets containing amphetamine on Jagger, and Robert Fraser with more of the same plus some heroin.

Before the police left, David, Robert and Mick were charged with possession, and the householder with allowing Redlands to be used for the consumption of the Acid King's cannabis. After *The News Of The World* had all but named the accused on a front page headlined 'DRUG SQUAD RAIDS POP STARS' PARTY' the following Sunday, Keith and Mick decided on temporary flight overseas, away from the prattle of media lingering outside recording studios and on the pavements outside the Stones' London dwellings, shamelessly gaping at the sash windows, some going as far as to press the doorbells.

It would be beyond the hacks' immediate powers to track the fugitives to Morocco to where Mick flew, and Keith – with Brian, Anita and three other friends – went by road, across France and Spain to catch the ferry from Malaga. Towards the close of the first day, however, Jones's intake of alcohol and marijuana in the back seat helped aggravate the asthma that had dogged him since childhood. Before they reached the Spanish border, he had checked in at a hospital where it was discovered that his eye-crossing coughs had caused both lungs to bleed. Urged to remain there for observation, Brian would, he said, join everybody in Morocco later. This proved a historic decision that was to affect the entire course of both the Stones' career and Jones' and Richards' lives.

During the night, Brian reconsidered and, wishing her to return to the hospital, sent one telegram after another to Anita in the hotel in central Spain where her and Keith's yawns at breakfast would indicate that neither had been in bed alone. With retrospective honesty, Anita would aver, 'By the time we reached Valencia, we could no longer resist each other. Keith spent the night in my room. In the morning, I realised – as did Keith – that we were creating an unmanageable situation – so we pulled back as best we could for the rest of the journey.'[1]

On arrival in Morocco too, the pair conducted themselves as best they could on the same just-friends terms as before, except for awkward lulls in pool-side conversations and split-second looks noticed by Mick, Brian, when he turned up, and other

British holidaymakers such as society photographer Cecil Beaton. His description of Richards' – and Jones's – seedy-flash flower-power attire is worth quoting: 'In eighteenth century suit, long black velvet coat and the tightest pants, everything is shoddy, poorly made, the seams burst. Keith himself had sewn his trousers, lavender and dull rose, with a band of badly-stitched leather dividing the two colours. Brian appears in white pants with a huge black square applied at the back. It is very smart in spite of the fact that the seams are giving way.'[14]

Keith was certain that Brian's nervous manner towards him was because he dreaded finding that his growing suspicions had substance. Fear, however, was deferring to stoic cynicism and then naked anger. 'Brian kept staring at Keith,' perceived Anita, 'I could sense the rage building up.'[1]

In the privacy of the bedroom, Brian's wrath exploded like shrapnel in a slanging match, unflattering comparisons to local prostitutes and blows rained on Anita that left her with visible minor injuries, as well as budgerigar eyes after the remainder of a sleepless night and the incessant sound of his voice.

The next day, Brian unzipped a scripted grin on an equally drawn face and tried not to betray his own distress, but 'when Keith saw what Brian had done to me, he got me aside and tried to console me. "I can't watch Brian do this to you any more," he said, "I'm going to take you back to London." I was terrified but exhilarated to be freeing myself from Brian's tyranny. I was more than ready to give that up, especially since I was now almost in love with Keith.'[1]

True love, however, didn't run smoothly, either then or later. On the subsequent Stones tour of Europe, hope stirred fleetingly in Brian's breast that he might win Anita back when Keith, allegedly, had a fling with another woman during the German leg. However, if Anita got wind of this episode, she came to terms with it as one of the perks of her new boyfriend's job – just as among its hazards was the gallery overflowing with press, fans and starstruck legal staff employed elsewhere in the building, who had come to watch the fun when Keith, Mick and this Robert person emphatically denied all charges at West Sussex Quarter Sessions on 27 June. Acid King David was absent, having fled the country to escape either justice or the revelation that he was a *News Of The World* fink.

Taking the witness stand after Fraser and Jagger had already been found guilty, Richards gave a remarkably cool and articulate account of himself, though he may have overplayed his hand as the anti-establishment young rock 'n' roller up against the ugly, short-haired old squares: 'When the prosecuting counsel asked me about chicks in nothing but fur rugs, I said, "I'm not concerned with your petty morals". They couldn't take that one.'[9]

It was almost a foregone conclusion that the Crown would enjoy a total victory. The ITV evening news was full of 'Mick Jagger and his guitarist Keith Richard'[15] being jailed respectively for three months and a year – with Keith receiving his sentence 'without expression'.[15] By the time the ITV bulletin was over, he'd be picking without relish at a meal that included toffee-coloured chips and congealing custard in Wormwood Scrubs as Prisoner No. 7855.

8 His Satanic Majesty

'In the studio, nobody was friendly, and everybody acted
funny.'   – *Ry Cooder*[1]

By nefarious means, surprisingly friendly fellow convicts offered
Keith cigarettes containing the very substance that had sent him
to gaol. He wouldn't have minded. If he was really going to be
banged up for a year, a supply of spliffs would help the time pass
quicker in an establishment where 'the food's awful, the wine list
is terribly limited, and the library is abysmal'.[2]

Beneath the wry shallowness, Richards was an
understandably shaken and downcast man, but his response to
the orderliness of prison life was made easier when, during the
prescribed counter-clockwise walk around the exercise yard the
next day, other inmates, drawing from their own experiences
with the law, filled his head surreptitiously with trumped-up
charges, victimisation, making an example and further theories
of how and why he'd ended up there, and how and why he'd be
out sooner rather than later. Keith was heartened further that
afternoon when a thunderous huzzah rent the building as, via a
workshop Tannoy, a Stones record was spun on pirate Radio
London, then awaiting its final hour when the Marine Offences
Act became law in August 1967.

Through the oratory skills of his barrister, Keith – like Mick
– would be free by dusk, awaiting an ultimately successful
appeal. Over the previous 24 hours, hundreds of teenagers had
demonstrated in Piccadilly Circus and outside the *News Of The*

World block, The Who's manager, Kit Lambert, placed an advertisement in a national daily objecting to Keith and Mick being 'treated as scapegoats for the drug problem',[3] and The Who themselves had knocked out a single, reviving 'The Last Time' and 'Under My Thumb', an *Aftermath* opus. Royalties from its three weeks in the lower reaches of the Top 50 were to be donated to Richards' and Jagger's legal costs.

The Stones had been disappointed, however, that help had not been forthcoming from more obvious resources, especially as, less than a month after the European tour, Brian Jones had also been busted. Afraid that Scotland Yard was lining him up for the next pounce, Andrew Oldham was in limbo in California, and was to resign as the group's manager by autumn.

Decca had forsaken Keith, Mick and Brian altogether. Certain company executives, despite finding Oldham and the Stones personally objectionable, had felt obliged to support their endeavours on disc in order to cater to a worldwide and, in many cases, equally repulsive fan base. This didn't extend, however, to pulling strings to get the insolent little nitwits out of trouble with the police.

Via Keith's principal drugs dealer, a huge bribe for a bent cop to render the concrete evidence (the cannabis and Jagger's pills), invalid fell on stony ground as well. Further attempts at extra-legal fixing, allied with whispered wisdom received in Wormwood Scrubs, 'destroyed once and for all my faith in the fairness and impartiality of the British justice system',[4] Richards was to groan after the case turned him into more than merely 'Mick Jagger's guitarist'.

Keen to find a new angle after years of the lead singer being the personification of the Stones, many journalists wondered whether Keith was just as worthy of repellent fascination on the quiet with his saturnine aspect and crow's-nest haircut, now slightly spiked like that of one of Procol Harum – very much the men of the moment with their 'A Whiter Shade Of Pale' vying with The Beatles' 'All You Need Is Love' and the Stones' 'We Love You'/'Dandelion' as the most plugged single on the dying Radio London's playlist.

Rush-released in August, the Stones' double A-side – notably 'Dandelion' – reflected a pixified musical scenario pertinent to the commercialisation of flower power that pervaded the summer charts. Cashing in quick that same month were The Flowerpot Men, a quartet of London session singers who, garbed in beads, chiffony robes and like regalia, mimed on *Top Of The Pops* to 'Let's Go To San Francisco', a paean to the city where it had all started – and where the blooms were now beginning to wilt. At Number Four, 'Let's Go To San Francisco' finished four positions higher than the Stones' 45 in the UK Top Ten.

Yet before such exercises in expediency came thick and fast, there had been fleeting moments when many had been convinced – as arch flower-child-*cum*-pop singer Donovan was – that God had 'seen all the ugliness that was being created and had chosen pop to be the great force of love and beauty'.[5] A similarly sweet petal from the lips of disc-jockey and *International Times* columnist John Peel was, 'There are sparrows and flowers and roses in my head. Sometimes, I don't have enough time to think of loving you. That is very wrong.'[6]

Keith Richards was genuinely in love, if not with everyone like Donovan and John Peel were, then with Anita Pallenberg. Though he was evasive when the subjects of wedding bells and babies reared up in interview, he was, flirtations on the road notwithstanding, a constant heart. 'Keith was a bit like Charlie,' affirmed Ian Stewart, 'Keith would find one girl and pretty much stick with her. Maybe a few here and there, but nothing like Brian and Bill, who went potty over birds.'[4]

Chief among Brian's seraglio these days was Linda Keith, but, however grotesque his exhibitions with her and other of his women – apparently, leading one of them into a party on a chain like a dog – he was fundamentally brokenhearted by Anita's deceit. There'd been consequent sly but vainglorious machinations to place her in such a position where she'd be unable to resist him when he turned on the little-boy-lost charm that had done the trick when they'd first met in Munich in 1965.

In Brian's fool's paradise, the final grand gesture took place when, following Pallenberg's completion in Italy of a prominent role in the science-fiction movie *Barbarella*, she and Keith arrived at the annual international film exposition in Cannes for the screening of *Mort Und Toschlag* for which she had acted a major part and Brian had composed the soundtrack. Benighted in the same hotel, Jones 'tried to engineer some scheme', glowered Richards. 'Previously, he had tried to engineer a reunion in Paris, but Anita wouldn't have it. During the première in Cannes, I just stayed away. Anita came back in tears because Brian had tried to beat her up.'[4]

Through Pallenberg and her contacts in the film world, Keith was given a cameo in *Michael Kohlhaus*, a flick starring her and David Warner, which was withdrawn soon after its general release in 1969 – and would have been lost anyway in the shadow of Anita's next role in *Performance*, for which Keith and Mick were to provide a song to accompany one of the scenes. Actually 'in the can' before *Michael Kohlhaus*, *Performance* was regarded by its investors as principally a vehicle for Jagger as a screen idol.

Jagger had also been central figure on the *trompe l'oeil* front cover as well as chief advocate of the musical content of *Their Satanic Majesties Request*, a Stones album issued in December 1967. In as much as 'We Love You'/'Dandelion' was a 'concept' single – with a segment of the former serving as coda for the latter – the LP was, theoretically, a continuous 'work' with little or no spaces between tracks, replete with segues; a reprise of the opening track; vague sustaining of a recurring mood and backwards-running tapes, funny noises and other clutter that disguised many essentially banal artistic perceptions.

That was okay by me – though I never acquired a copy until one surfaced, scratched and scuffed, in a car-boot sale decades later. With retrospective honesty, nevertheless, Keith thought that 'basically, *Satanic Majesties* was a load of crap. It was really almost done semi-comatose, sort of "Do we really have to make an album?"'[4]

How could he criticise an item of merchandise that was assured a gold disc before its conception, let alone its release? Various of the Stones' contemporaries, however, were struggling. After 'The Last Time'/'Under My Thumb', had risen no higher than Number 44, The Who could no longer take chart strikes for granted. Furthermore, that a typical Hollies fan was either opposed or insensible to experiment was demonstrated when their ambitious 'King Midas In Reverse' crawled wretchedly to the edge of the Top 20 while its follow-up, 'Jennifer Eccles', the group's artistic nullity, shot into the Top Ten. As for The Downliners Sect, engagement fees were often a minus amount following deductions, and 'Do you know anywhere we can sleep tonight?' became a frequent question asked of hangers-on in frowzy dressing rooms.

The Pretty Things' living still depended on earnings from the road too, though they were amenable to playing for just expenses on a stage erected within the barricades of a sit-in at London's Goldsmith College at the request of Germaine Greer, then a professor of English there. With New Left radicalism and the war in Vietnam the common denominators, kaftans had been mothballed as their former wearers followed the crowd to such tub-thumping events as well as unmistakably violent anti-war marches and moratoriums.

When pressed about the far away hostilities and like inflammable topics, Keith wouldn't join together – as Mick did – with a militant mob outside the US Embassy, but he was active after a detached pop-starrish fashion in verbally endorsing pacifism and dissident popular opinion, while enquiring, 'How many times can they use those words – justice, freedom? It's like margarine. You can package and sell that too.'[7] More pointed anger was directed at Decca, who, so Keith understood, were ploughing back monies amassed through record sales into its radar division – which made parts for air force bombers in Vietnam.

For all his political reserve in public, Richards was often quite loquacious when expressing his views among familiars in Chelsea's Baghdad House, a favoured restaurant until whirring cameras began heralding the arrival of professional celebrities. It was there that Dick Taylor, soon to fly The Pretty Things' nest for several years, met his old mates Keith and Mick for the first time in ages. Of the two, Richards seemed to Dick to be the most changed by the aeons that had passed since Little Boy Blue And The Blue Boys: 'Mick always had affectations of speech – especially during his Cockney phase – but he was essentially a well-spoken grammar school boy. Keith had a rougher accent, but suddenly he was all la-di-da: "How fabulous! Lovely to see you!" – just like Alexis Korner rather than Keith, the barrow-boy-type I knew of old.'

As well as European film directors and fine-art connoisseurs like Eton-educated Robert Fraser, Richards was also keeping company with 'preppy' North Americans such as Ingram Cecil Connor III, the scion of a Florida orange-merchandising dynasty – albeit one blighted by his father's suicide, his mother's alcoholism and his sister's commitment to a mental institution. Moreover, though he won a scholarship to study theology at Harvard, Ingram did not graduate, preferring to take his chances as an all-round country-and-western musician, using the stage alias 'Gram Parsons'.

In 1968, as a member of The Byrds, Gram was the prime mover behind the group's stylistic transition from jingle-jangling 'acid-folk' to the yee-hah boots-and-saddles exuberance of 1968's *Sweetheart Of The Rodeo*, an album pre-empted vaguely by *John Wesley Harding*, Bob Dylan's plain-and-simple new morning, recorded in Nashville. Of similarly insidious impact, *Music From Big Pink* by Dylan's backing Band was a True West blend of electric folklore that had been nurtured over years in hick Canadian dancehalls with Ronnie Hawkins, the Tony Sheridan to their Beatles.

While he liked *Music From Big Pink*, Keith was to be disappointed after he arrived by helicopter on 1969's August bank holiday weekend to hear The Band precede Dylan's headlining spot at the second Isle of Wight Festival. 'It was like they were just playing the records, and at a fairly low volume with very clear sound. I like some distortion, especially if something starts happening on stage.'[8]

He was more partial to The Wailing Wailers, fronted by a certain Bob Marley, who were bruited as a Jamaican variant on The Rolling Stones via a more indigenous – and dangerous – sound than the isolated hits of The Migil Five, Millie and, more recently, Prince Buster and Desmond Dekker.

Rock 'n' roll revival was in the air too as Bill Haley and Buddy Holly reissues sneaked into the Top 50, and students' union entertainment officers rubbed their chins over provincial combos led by backdated Teddy Boys such as Crazy Cavan and Shakin' Stevens. Across the Atlantic, the ilk of Sha Na Na, Flash Cadillac and Cat Mother were also carrying a torch for the 1950s.

The general post-psychedelic rejection of musical insights that weren't immediately comprehensible reared up too in the Stones' new 45, 'Jumpin' Jack Flash'. It was as unvarnished and as *au naturel* as it was possible to be by marrying a return to the Craw Daddy primaeval to advanced technology without too much premeditated kow-towing to either 'meaningful' lyrics or standard changes within a three-chord structure. Into the bargain, rather than lose the drive inherent in the take used, a jarring couple of bars from the guitars in the middle instrumental passage were retained as an 'irritant factor'.

Pete Townshend was so excited by 'Jumpin' Jack Flash' that he advised recalling the buzz you got the first time you heard it as an aid to reaching a state of meditative bliss. 'It's the one that I would immediately go to if I wanted to approach a state of nirvana,' agreed Keith. 'The feeling's one of exhilaration. As soon as I play that riff, something happens in your stomach. It's an amazing, superhuman feeling. An explosion would be the best way to describe it.'[4]

With the single at Number One at home, Three in the USA, Two in Australia and at comparable positions in all other chart territories, it was clear that the paring down to just vocals, guitars, bass and drums, plus keyboards and minor percussion where needed, met with public approval. It made sense, therefore, to expect the same of the interrelated LP, *Beggars Banquet* (for which 'Jumpin' Jack Flash' was first intended). Employed on both the single and the album, one technique developed by Keith was taping an acoustic guitar, with attached magnetic pick-up, through an amplifier onto his cassette recorder – one of the first privately purchased such machines in Britain – with so much overspill that it sounded electric. On transference to the eight-track mixing desk in Olympic Sound, the studio now favoured whenever the Stones recorded in London, it also lent a gritty quality to finished products such as topical 'Street Fighting Man' – on which the only solid-body instrument heard was the bass, also thrummed by Richards.

On other *Beggars Banquet* tracks, Keith was also crossing what outsiders had understood to be another demarcation line by inserting bottleneck (or slide) guitar, once Brian Jones's exclusive preserve, for which it was necessary to tune to an open chord. Most commonly, it was G major, requiring the removal of the lower string so that the dominant wouldn't, well, dominate.

During the transition between *Satanic Majesties* and *Beggars Banquet*, the conducting of such experiments had 'rejuvenated my enthusiasm for playing guitar – because you'd put your fingers where you thought they'd go, and you'd get accidents happening.'[4] Rather than Brian's direct absorption of Elmore James, Muddy Waters and other blues exponents, Keith preferred the more academic approach of Gram Parsons – and, more so, Los Angeles-born Ry Cooder, a bottleneck – and mandolin – virtuoso, fresh from Captain Beefheart's Magic Band, who was then in London to assist with incidental music to *Performance*.

Invited to Redlands, Cooder was initially flattered but not quite comfortable by the close attention his host paid to his picking. As well as 'taking Ry Cooder for all I could get',[1] Keith escorted him into Olympic one spring evening in 1969 to shimmer mandolin on a C&W-tinged arrangement of Robert Johnson's 'Love In Vain', earmarked for the next Stones album, *Let It Bleed*. With some bitterness at the time, Cooder would claim co-authorship of Richards' and Jagger's 'Honky Tonk Women' – and its 'Country Honk' derivative – that were both recorded in the same period. Later, he came to terms with it: 'It's of zero importance. There's nothing I can say about that without looking like a chump. If you want to know, ask Keith. The experience with the Stones showed me one thing – which is that if you don't advance yourself, you'll find yourself left in the dust.'[1]

This grievance put the tin-lid on any possibility of Cooder, a home-loving sort anyway, remaining on a short list of possible successors to Brian Jones, whose tenure as a Rolling Stone would end shortly after his cursory contribution to *Let It Bleed*'s 'Midnight Rambler' on 16 May 1969. As well as the business in Morocco annihilating any cosy pretensions about the Stones as a five-man brotherhood, Brian's seemingly perpetual drug-clouded state since was mirrored in an increasing morosity as he was pushed further into the background by Mick and, particularly, Keith, who was now very much 'in charge of recording sessions, more or less, in an oblique way', according to Ian Stewart. 'He doesn't march into the studio and say, "Right! It's going to be this, that and the other." He just kicks off into something, and most people follow him. He usually decides how each song is going to shape up.'[4]

All that remained of Brian's stolen vocational inheritance were scrapings such as his shaky and slender hand in December 1968's *Rolling Stones' Rock 'N' Roll Circus*, a subsequently cancelled televisual spectacular with a sequential pot-pourri of clowns, gymnasts, fire-eaters, a tiger – and music that mashed up blues, rock, ballads and items that beggared precise categorisation. The show closed with a performance by the Stones, whose musicianship was slammed by Ian Anderson, singing flautist in one of the support acts, Jethro Tull, with specific reference to Brian.

Jones had been afforded a kind of forlorn satisfaction via hearsay that sections of the *Performance* script requiring sexual intimacy between Anita and Mick had gone beyond dramatic simulation, Pallenberg excusing this as 'method acting'. Richards had been sulking gently as the evil hour approached when his 'chick' was actually going to cavort between bedsheets with his best pal, but alarmist reports about the two actually doing the dirty deed for real were too much for Keith, brooding in a parked car outside the house where the cameras were set up.

Was it the karma for his brief *amour* with Marianne? Consumed with at least a glimmer of what Jones must have felt, Richards expressed his resentment by making 'Memo From Turner', his and Mick's composition for the film, sound so amateurish when he deigned to turn up at the long-delayed session with the Stones that session musicians – including Ry Cooder – had to be hired for the difficult task of layering a more acceptable backing onto a busy Jagger vocal, now isolated from the original effort.

More dangerous, if private, comforts during a year beset with too many traumas were Keith's first escapes into reveries induced by cocktails of cocaine – and its sister narcotic, heroin. He imagined then that he could give it up any time he liked.

9 The Demon Brother

'People were dropping like flies. It was nothing to wake up once a week, and hear so-and-so's gone.'

– Keith Richards[1]

In June 1969, it was announced that The Rolling Stones, with 21-year-old guitarist Mick Taylor replacing Brian Jones, would play a show in London, that – defying belief – would be free of charge! The buckshee bash was pencilled in by organisers Blackhill Enterprises for Saturday 5 July beside the Serpentine, the artificial lake in Hyde Park.

So often did such altruistic happenings pock the alternative culture's social calendar in post flower-power England that reaction when scanning billing in *Time Out* or *International Times* had shifted from a cynical 'Yes, but how much is it to get in?' to a jaded 'Hmmm, is that all that's on this time?' Nevertheless, depending on what Sunday newspaper landed on your doormat, audience estimates for the Stones would range from 200,000 to 750,000. However exaggerated, it was certainly the largest assembly for any cultural event ever accommodated by the capital. 'I can't stop dreaming about it,' exclaimed Keith Richards a month later in the *New Musical Express*, 'It has to be the biggest crowd I've ever seen. They were the stars of the show – like some massive religious gathering on the shores of the Ganges.'[2]

There was, indeed, an element of ritual to the occasion. Only a day before there'd been talk of cancellation out of respect for

Brian, who'd died suddenly on Thursday. Keith's feelings about him ran too deep for simple analysis, but it was decided to turn the event into a send-off for Jones with an oration from Jagger immediately before a dispelling of the collective grief as the Stones launched into a set that, heard on the *Stones In The Park* video 14 years on, appalled me with its careless tonality – though my teenage self hadn't been aware that anything was wrong when the notes were first hung in the air – with Keith admitting, 'I was a bit shaky at first, but then I started enjoying myself.'[2]

After a fashion, so did I when joining in the booing of The Battered Ornaments, who had the irksome task of preceding the Stones onto the boards. The Ornaments' avant-garde jazz, like the better-received King Crimson's earlier slot, demonstrated a more commanding instrumental precision than anything the bill-toppers could produce. Next, while the Stones kept everyone waiting in the heat, some half-wit near the guest enclosure begged a now-famous Edgar Broughton – the bloke from Tony And The Talons and The Original Roadrunners – to get up onstage and give 'em his celebrated audience participation number, 'Out Demons Out'. 'We don't mind if the Stones do one less number,' the supplicant generalised airily, indicating the sweating multitudes behind him. He wasn't very popular. Any other artiste's most rabble-rousing showstopper could not be allowed to subtract a split-second from even the lousiest Stones presentation.

They kicked off with a number that had been a turntable fixture at Brian's final earthly home, 'I'm Yours And I'm Hers' by Johnny Winter, a boss-eyed, albino Texan who had become a luminary of the late 1960s 'blues boom' after an LP he'd recorded for an obscure regional company impressed a *Rolling Stone* journalist. The resulting eulogy in 1968 catapulted Johnny from local renown to headlining at New York's Scene club and the prestigious Fillmore East. He was, however, annoyed when a compilation of old recordings was issued in the same month as an 'official' second album. Among enthusiast listeners were John Lennon and Keith Richards. Each was to pen a song for Winter – respectively, 'Rock 'N' Roll People' and 'Silver Train'.

Buoyed by such big-time approbation and his own self-belief ('In my own mind, I was the best white blues player around'[3]), Winter plunged into a lucrative booking schedule on the early 1970s rock circuit – including Woodstock and 1970's Bath Festival. At each, another *nouveau* white blues act, Canned Heat, were well received too, having established themselves with the global bestseller, 'On The Road Again' from *Boogie With Canned Heat* – on which the trademark droning rhythm of 'Refried Hockey Boogie' occupied an entire side. 'Goin' Up The Country' and 1970's 'Let's Work Together' were also chart-busters, and the band became as well known as a reliable draw at outdoor festivals. That said, the taped results as vibrations hanging in the air many mornings after were okay but not brilliant – and, as you'll be told by anyone who has encountered Canned Heat on the boards before or since, that, like the Stones by the Serpentine, you had to have been there.

Signifying pop's growing internationalism, among those passing through Canned Heat's ranks later was Stan Webb, whose Chicken Shack had also made hay during this wave of mass interest in electric blues. 'We were one of the first bands with great stacks of Marshall amps behind us,' recalled Stan with quiet pride. 'We were so bloody loud, we could – and did – get away with murder, doing a mix of blues and R&B, featuring lots of Muddy Waters and Howlin' Wolf.'[4]

Too hot for the Midlands to hold, the ensemble had been signed in 1967 to Blue Horizon, a company founded by former Decca recording manager Mike Vernon, who regarded them as 'probably the most solid Stones-type Chicago blues band of them all'.[4] After 1968's *Forty Blue Fingers Freshly Packed Ready To Serve* left its mark in the UK album list at a gratifying Number 12, a cover of Etta James's mordant 'I'd Rather Go

Blind' was conveniently high in the Top Ten when, following Hyde Park, the Stones prepared to return to touring after a two-year lay-off with a repertoire that, in part, nodded at the blues boom with genre examples that had poked out of *Beggars Banquet* and the forthcoming *Let It Bleed*.

Keith, however, wasn't quite ready to tear himself away from his new London abode, 3 Cheyne Walk, on the opposite side of the road to Mick (with whom, apparently, the *Performance* hatchet had now been buried). It was to this oak-panelled 18th-century town house that Keith drove his and Anita's first child after delivery on 10 August at King's College Hospital. Named Marlon – after Brando – the boy had survived a pregnancy blighted by a road accident, the second of many involving his father. An outcome of a misjudged exit from a Sussex roundabout in a vintage Mercedes was treatment for shock and a fractured collarbone for Anita.

For a while after the birth, sedate domesticity was the order of the day, expressed by Keith in the beginnings of a countrified *lied* entitled 'Wild Horses' that 'couldn't drag me away' from this protective bubble as he stole nervous glances at the increasing depth into which the Stones would plunge if they failed to live up to a selfish public's expectations now that five weeks of confirmed dates in the USA, starting in Colorado on 1 November, had sold out within hours.

The building tension was exacerbated by a scent of diabolical practices emanating from both the group's songwriting hub and as the legacy of some of Brian's and Anita's antics when they were together. As well as *Satanic Majesties* and 'Sympathy For The Devil' on *Beggars Banquet*, there were undenied rumours of liaisons with black and white witches – and Kenneth Anger, a former Hollywood child star, who, now in middle life, styled himself 'The Most Monstrous Movie Maker In The Underground'.

Modelling both his private life and public persona on that of 'Great Beast' Aleister Crowley, Anger's livelihood and reputation depended on bleak cult movies such as 1947's homosexual gang rape fantasy *Fireworks*; *Lord Shiva's Dream*, a coded titular reference to LSD, renamed *Inauguration Of The Pleasure Dome* and 1963's apocalyptic *Scorpio Rising*, betraying a fascination with the books of Dennis Wheatley. His social circle was commensurate with this, embracing the likes of Anais Nin, whose prose poem-*cum*-novel, *The House Of Incest*, provided the libretto for post-serialist composer Edgard Varese's murkiest work, *Nocturnal*, and, since 1967, Anita Pallenberg and her pop star intimates.

When a guest at Redlands, Anger volunteered to officiate, after suggesting in vain that Richards and Pallenberg wed in a pagan ceremony either in the grounds or on Hampstead Heath at dawn.[5] He was also to insert footage from the Hyde Park extravaganza into *Invocation Of My Demon Brother*, and would visualise Keith as Beelzebub in *Lucifer Rising*, another flick then in pre-production.

Phantasmagoria had been infiltrating Richards' musical vocabulary since first he listened to, say, Robert Johnson's 'Hellhound On My Trail' and his Faustian 'Me And The Devil Blues' plus like ditties from the spectrum of black music, whether Screaming Jay Hawkins in the badlands of rock 'n' roll or Peetie Wheatstraw, who flourished in the pre-war Deep South, and named himself at various times 'The Devil's Son-in-Law' and 'The High Sheriff of Hell'.

Some of Keith's more piquant netherworld excursions since may have been via LSD, but as 1970 approached these manifested themselves mainly in flashback as hallucinogenics became less popular than heroin as a muse. 1969's chart debut by David Bowie, 'Space Oddity', was seen in some quarters as a paean to the stuff – which was taking gradual if unknowing possession of Keith during the US expedition.

With Brian out of the way, and Mick Taylor seemingly as meek as a lamb, Richards, onstage with one of the newfangled transparent Plexiglas guitars, was becoming more than one of the four human walls of the cavorting Mick-as-Jumpin' Jack Flash's padded cell. Previously, many onlookers hadn't given him that much notice, but, while Jagger wasn't yet to wave him in to hog the central microphone, he was switching to acoustic and seating himself on one of two stools brought on to enable him and Mick to duet folk-club style on 'Prodigal Son', an ancient blues excavated for *Beggars Banquet*, while the other three took a breather.

During more typical Stones fare, the interaction between Richards and Taylor revealed a stronger differentiation between lead and rhythm guitars than there'd been under the old regime of Brian's and Keith's fretboard counterpoint – so much so that tidy-minded (or lazy) journalists were lauding Keith's chord-flaying as much as they were his and Taylor's most dazzling solos. Suddenly, a rhythm guitarist no longer skulked in grey mediocrity beyond the main spotlight while the other fellow stupefied listeners with his note-bending dexterity. 'Without Keith's rhythm guitar, there'd be no Rolling Stones,' declared Jack Nitzsche, a longtime studio associate, 'What Keith does is play guitar without trying to be flash. It's all taste. Keith doesn't make a lot of faces.'[6]

Unheeded was the lad himself's cry, 'I didn't say I was a rhythm guitarist. Other people made my reputation for me.'[6] He was, nevertheless, the unintended hero of the hour – as far as there was one – when the tour concluded with an attempt to recapture that Serpentine magic with a free concert at Altamont, a racetrack under more usual circumstances, just an hour's drive from San Francisco. With the benefit of hindsight, the first time in England should have been the only time because, while the Stones delivered more routinely solid goods than at Hyde Park, Altamont would be remembered by Keith as 'chaos. I wouldn't say frightening, but definitely high in adrenaline. I was wondering who the hell was running the joint. Five hundred thousand people, guys are getting stabbed, the Hell's Angels are out of it on acid and Thunderbird wine. The only way you could cool it was by facing them down. The one thing you can't do is give way to fear or intimidation.'[7]

The performances of the acts that preceded them soundtracked beatings-up – and, within the Stones' range of vision, someone was actually killed. Bestial faces got eyefuls of unofficial spectator sport as an 18-year-old black youth, later identified as Meredith Hunter, squirmed and screamed with pain and panic in a forest of kicking motorbike boots and sawn-off pool cues.

From a distance of years, the central figures of this and other of the uglier commotions at Altamont were held to be members of local chapters of the Hell's Angels that Keith mentioned, hired as 'security' because it was reckoned that the invidious motorcycle brotherhood with its Nazi regalia had a special rapport with equally non-conformist hippies. All that 'love and peace' nonsense in 1967 might have grasped the wrong end of the stick, but the stick still existed.

That's as may be, but a growing cluster of Angels were to be under the impression that they now had licence to mill about on the boards, close enough to touch the official entertainment, project psychopathic thousand-yard stares into the crowd and exact bloody reprisals against anyone who dared do as little as, say, stare back. Hemmed in by their so-called protectors, the Stones resolved tacitly to quit the stage, the site and the district as swiftly as possible.

During one slow moment of a nerve-wracking set, Keith was distracted by fans subjected to arbitrary manhandling so exultantly brutal that he rebuked the attackers from the footlights. His precise words were, 'If those cats don't stop fighting, we're going to split' – and there'd be a spreading tale that Sonny Barger, an Angel of high office, levelled a pistol at him and barked, 'Start playing or you're dead!'[8]

While this may have been merely one of the self-created myths that adhered to the fearsome Barger, Keith retained clearer pictures of 'the actual getaway: everyone running up this hill to a hovering helicopter. It was like Vietnam. You had to jump and climb up this rope-ladder, trying to make sure you got the women on there first.'[7]

With another lesson learned – 'not to try and do anything like that again'[9] – Keith confirmed with the other Stones that proceeds from television and film coverage of Altamont should go to an orphanage for Vietnamese orphans. It was the least they could do.

10 The Wild Horseman

'Rock 'n' roll is big business, you know. Musicians who find themselves suddenly the focal point of millions and millions of dollars neither have the time nor inclination to be able to look after it properly.'

– Keith Richards [1]

Artificial snow cascaded onto entering ticket holders at the Strand Lyceum on 21 December 1969 when the Stones played their first 'home games' – a matinée and a soirée there and a week earlier at the Saville Theatre – since Hyde Park. However demonstrative their altruism on that summer's day, the purpose of these sold-out concerts was the same as that of any other rock group – to make a monetary killing.

There was also a tinge of a prodigals' return. Though the corrupted endeavour that was Altamont had been represented as an overall success in most of Britain's national newspapers, a harsher truth had resonated from an edition of *Rolling Stone* devoted almost entirely to the event. Not a page went by without some vestige of blame sticking to the Stones.

This report, however, had only just leaked into London, and the majority of the Saville and Lyceum crowds hadn't understood the full bitterness of what had occurred. Therefore, if there was any rancorous puzzlement, the Stones were still able to exact their customary submission from whoever hadn't wanted to like them among the post-Woodstock flurry of long print dresses, pre-faded Levis embroidered with butterfly or mushroom motifs, clogs, bell-bottomed loon pants, cloche hats, grandad vests, air-force greatcoats and, even in the winter chill, stars-and-stripes singlets revealing underarm hair.

Here was condolence for the terrible end of the Stones' journey across North America: the acclamation of the Great British Public. That made up for the fallout from Altamont and, in the New Year, the first Stones bootleg, *Live R Than You'll Ever Be*, taped at Oakland Coliseum, the third stop on the US trek. It defied every known copyright law, but sold in sufficient quantities to qualify for a gold disc. Such recordings had been common in jazz circles for years, but had come into pop prominence in 1969 when *Great White Wonder*, an illicit Bob Dylan double album, opened the floodgates for countless more items of this type, so much so that *Rolling Stone* took to reviewing some as seriously as if they were legitimate releases.

I bought a *Live R Than You'll Ever Be* from the suitcase of a pavement trader on Oxford Street. On thrusting it onto my Dansette, I was surprised at the precise and forceful fidelity – especially when set against the questionable clarity of similar merchandise not meant for John Citizen's ears. Indeed, it compared so favourably with even the official *Get Yer Ya-Yas Out* – from New York – that it fuelled a pungent rumour that the Stones themselves had been responsible for their own bootleg. Yet, while topping the domestic chart and peaking nearly as high across the Atlantic, *Get Yer Ya-Yas Out* had been subject to much fine-tuning and ironing out of faults in Olympic to the degree that Keith calculated that as much time was spent on this in-concert effort as on some of the studio albums.

Another spin-off from the tour was *Gimmie Shelter*, which Keith had wanted to title *Naughty Ladies' 70*. Centred mainly on Altamont, it was praised for its technical qualities and, while winning no Oscars, remained in general circulation for far longer than the other big rock movie of the turning decade, *Zabriskie Point*. This slow-moving fantasy of wonderful young people running away from over-civilised old squares was 'modern' enough to seem dated now, but is pertinent to this discussion because its soundtrack included *Let It Bleed*'s 'You Got The Silver', Keith's first true lead vocal on disc, along with tracks by The Grateful Dead, Roy Orbison and Pink Floyd.

The aimless and downbeat mood of *Zabriskie Point* was but one symptom of mopish post-Swinging Sixties doldrums. Another was the drab uniformity of the early 1970s school of singing songwriters that infested both college bedsits and the hit parade. With all the charisma of Warhol's soup tins, solemn James Taylor, precious Elton John, twee Melanie or someone like them would whinge 'beautiful' cheesecloth-and-denim morosities, catching the general tenor of the bland 'Woodstock Generation' –whose anthem was Simon and Garfunkel's piteous 'Bridge Over Troubled Water'; who flocked to see *Zabriskie Point*; who hung on every nuance of the high-pitched quavering of Neil Young. No Mick Jaggerings were necessary. All you had to do onstage was sit on a stool, sing to your guitar and beam a small, sad smile every now and then to quietly attentive onlookers, so bound up in yourself that every tiny occurrence or emotion was worth relaying in song to the whole world.

In retrospect, the chasm between 'You Got The Silver' – penned, apparently, for Anita during the *Performance* shooting – and, say, a piece of doggerel by Melanie about tuning her guitar or David Crosby about *almost* cutting his thinning hair was far from unbreachable. Had the Stones gone sour on him then, Keith might have had a walkover as a singer-songwriter via an album or two of more of the same.

Keith was also well placed to profit from the commercial viability of a less mannered and artistically self-centred strain of rock impregnated with country and western's lyrical preoccupations and melodic appeal. Yet before the translation of C&W into a late 20th-century commentary on the aspirations of middle America, today's Dolly Parton compact disc consumer might have once proffered the excuse, 'I just had the radio on. I wasn't actually listening to it.'

'Listening to it' used to suggest association with uneducated, bigoted rednecks, descendants of the Wild West pioneers, and still caricatured as sectarian, unsophisticated and anti-intellectual. Then the most unfashionable and right-wing genre in pop, C&W had been a breeding ground for blue-collar sloganising, inciting suspicion of labour unions and antagonism towards pacifists and hippies now as well as commies, niggers and queers. Even in 1970, a Houston radio station had been twice firebombed by some good ol' boys who begged to differ with its radical anti-draft slant.

Nevertheless, taking their cue from the popularity of 'spaghetti westerns' and Nashville's spellbinding gaudiness, multitudinous licenced premises of the early 1970s had been transformed into parodies of Dodge City saloons. Barging through the swinging half-doors of an Edinburgh pub or Auckland bar, you'd bump into Calamity Jane lookalikes and stetsoned quaffers of Southern Comfort. Belying daytime guises as janitors or computer programmers, conversations would be peppered with Deep South slang – 'mess of grits' for 'plate of food' – picked up from Merle Haggard albums. On a nicotine-clouded stage, the band cranked out 'Okie From Muskogee,' 'Crystal Chandelier' and 'Polk Salad Annie'. If these mightn't have made the charts, they were as well known as many that had.

In common with Gram Parsons' Byrds, Bob Dylan, Neil Young, Ringo Starr and ex-Monkee Mike Nesmith had all 'gone country' too. Furthermore, Jerry Lee Lewis had risen anew as a C&W star, following a hit with 1968's 'Another Time Another Place'. That same year, Johnny Cash, described as 'the Keith Richards of country music'[2] after he'd assumed Hank Williams' crown as a drug-addled booker's risk, had earned the approbation of the hippie sub-culture for a professional liaison with Dylan and a televised concert before inmates of San Quentin penitentiary. The discerning Frank Zappa declared himself a Cash fan too.

While respective audiences were becoming less biased against one or the other, Keith had discussed possible fusions of country and classic rock with Gram Parsons while the latter was still a Byrd, initially during a lengthy debate one evening in Blaises. With its blending of cowboy pessimism and Victorian broadness of gesture, someone argued, what else was country but white man's blues? 'It was a logical step for The Rolling Stones to get into country music,' acknowledged Parsons, 'because they've always been well into the old blues since they first began.'[3]

During the same boozy conversation, it transpired too that Parsons was unhappy about The Byrds' forthcoming dates in apartheid-riven South Africa. 'On the spur of the moment, he decided to leave the band,' recalled Keith, 'so I had to put him up. We would get stoned, sit around with two guitars or a piano, and be the happiest kids in the sandbox.'[4] Coming with the territory was Gram's friend, Phil Kaufman, who ran the Executive Nanny Service, a security firm who were to be employed by The Rolling Stones.

Kaufman had also served as road manager for The Flying Burrito Brothers, formed by Parsons and other ex-Byrds, who had been among the support acts at Altamont. Sometimes he'd accompany Gram and Keith – and Anita – during nights in Southern California's High Desert, watching out for extraterrestrials. Many hours passed with no signs from outer space, unless hallucinogenically induced amid the often surreal landscapes of this arcadia of desert bloom and sun-dappled woodland that was becoming lost in an encroaching urban sprawl spreading from Los Angeles. Yet the area was on a par with Gauguin's South Sea island or Byron's Italy in its potential to inspire greatness or at least accommodate it, and it's feasible that 'Wild Horses' – to be a highlight of the next Stones LP,

Sticky Fingers and, before that, 1970's *Deluxe*, the second Flying Burrito Brothers' album – was completed there.

Parsons was present when three *Sticky Fingers* pieces were recorded at rural Alabama's trendy eight-track Muscle Shoals complex – 'very laid-back and relaxed', said Leon Russell. [5] The previous November, Russell, pianist on 'Live With Me', had introduced saxophonist Bobby Keyes to Richards (who, coincidentally, shared the same birthday). So began the infiltration of self-styled 'supersidemen' into the Stones' cabal. Every pop generation has, by its very nature, thrown up a self-contained privileged caste, but none was more insufferably smug as that faction of Los Angeles studio musicians also nicknamed 'the blue-eyed soul school'. That faintly sickening word 'funky' was used to describe the economic and squeaky-clean tightness of their rhythm section, but they couldn't accomplish what the old beat groups, for all their naivety and errors, had committed to tape instinctively.

Exchanging smirks across the console with ol' Leon, it was as if rock 'n' roll couldn't be played in any other way or with any other people than that elite tinged with a complacent snobbery about who was or wasn't worthy of their highly waged attention. Keyes and trumpeter Jim Price found it convenient to take up British residency to fulfil a selective work schedule that blossomed from pot-boiling sessions with relative unknowns like Third World War and Audience to assisting Billy Preston on his chart-busting 'That's The Way God Planned It' (on which Keith helped too); George Harrison, Preston's producer, on his own *All Things Must Pass* triple album, and proudly augmenting The Rolling Stones on the first tour *sur le continent* since 1967.

After thuggish North America, an excursion to dear old Europe should have been a mere bagatelle, but, two days after the first evening in Helsinki on 2 September 1970 passed without incident, the stage was invaded in Stockholm. Next, 50 youths were arrested before the show even started at Berlin's

Deutschlandhalle; several policemen required first aid outside the Olympia in Paris, and only tear gas could disperse 2,000 gatecrashers in Milan. It was as if James Taylor, Neil Young and Melanie had never happened.

As well as the ambles down Memory Lane and excerpts from *Let It Bleed*, the Stones were giving 'em no less than three Chuck Berry revivals and unfamiliar items from the album yet to come – including 'Bitch', earmarked as the single with Keyes and Price punching out Keith's four-bar riff, both in ragged unison with his fretting and to underpin his extrapolated solo between the final verse and the coda.

Keith would be all but inaudible during 'Moonlight Mile', the finale of an album that was a chronological and geographic ragbag, containing as it did, say, these backing tracks from Muscle Shoals and those overdubs at Olympic. The latest compositions had been routined in the Mobile at 'Stargroves', Mick's spread in Newbury over spring 1970, but 'Sister Morphine' dated from mid-1968.

Just as Ry Cooder may have felt he deserved a writing credit for 'Honky Tonk Women', and Mick Taylor for 'Moonlight Mile', so Marianne Faithfull claimed authorship of lyrics offered when Richards and Jagger were tinkering with the slow but captivating melody of 'Sister Morphine'. Smelling of hospitals, the song pictures a fragile junkie on a ward mattress after an arrival to the agitated clang of an ambulance bell.

A sense of longing as much as wretchedness also permeates the atmosphere. Though Keith found the emotional detachment to allow its selection for *Sticky Fingers*, 'Sister Morphine' was closer to the bone than it had once been. Though not yet breakneck, his – and Anita's – slide into heroin dependency had become unstoppable. 'I think part of the reason they submerged themselves in drugs,' theorised Marianne, 'was because they were trying to punish themselves for what they had done to Brian.'[6] Richards himself, however, ascribed it to 'coming off the road and dealing with the withdrawal and expenditure of energy that does it. I just haven't got any brakes. I was still so hyper – and I found that smack made it very much easier for me to slow down, very smoothly and gradually.'[1]

During these days, Keith's only contact with real life out in Dullsville was through narcotics dealers, gofers, chauffeurs, managers and bodyguards. The rest of us, it seemed, didn't count. Unaware too that a metaphorical pistol was being aimed at the very heart of the Stones by the Inland Revenue, Keith may have imagined that his wealth was so incalculable that he could afford to be a junkie, even as the queues lengthened outside dole offices and, in the teeth of a paralysing wave of national strikes, Britain's Labour government faced defeat in the summer's General Election.

Keeping pace with the pervading economic chaos, The Pretty Things weren't much of a group anymore, following a US tour in a lower league than their Stones compeers in the 'adult-orientated' rock hierarchy. 'It was a bit like doing a medicine show,' explained Phil May. 'We never knew what the venue was going to be until we turned up – from strip joints to ballrooms to ice rinks. In one tumbleweed town, we played in the Vixens' Den which was connected to this other club, the Foxes' Den, a strip joint, which played alternate shows. We had to do five sets a day. The birds would come and watch us in their negligees, and then we'd come and watch them. We shared the top floor of this hotel with them too.'

Bad boys attracted bad girls, among them a certain Nancy Spungeon from Philadelphia, whose parents were appalled on returning home to find their teenage daughter entertaining the Things in a manner peculiar to herself around the family swimming pool. 'They freaked out,' laughed Phil, 'She was only *trying* to be a groupie then.'

Spungen was to become notorious for her skills in evading the most stringent security barriers to impose herself on her idols

– including, apparently, Keith Richards, who was now as concerned that local narcotics dealers could contrive a network from the outside to sell their wares.

He had become quite a drugs connoisseur, recognising, for example, that LSD was rarely as pure as it had been in the mid-1960s. These days, it tended to be mixed with amphetamine. Some unscrupulous pushers even adulterated it with Ajax or Vim scourer.

Keith's interest in business affairs, however, was far less intense, although his years in the music industry had fostered in him a grasp of financial technicalities that, if opinionated, was less hesitant than most. As the expiry date of the Decca contract – 31 July 1970 – had crept closer, rumour had darkened to a certainty that the Stones were not going to re-sign, owing partly to what they saw as avaricious vacillation over perceived royalty discrepancies. Needless to say, Decca refuted this sullying of its good name, but swallowing its ire, sent representatives to join other major labels submitting their bids to one of the hottest properties in showbusiness.

That the metaphorical weather vane was turning in the direction of Atlantic Records had been indicated in April when Keith tagged along with Ahmet Ertegun, the firm's goateed supremo, and his brother Neshui when they visited the Speakeasy to catch a performance by Screaming Lord Sutch, the latest acquisition by a company that had been a bystander during the British Invasion, buoyed as it was by a bevy of hit-making black soul singers before seizing The Spencer Davis Group in 1966.

More recently, Led Zeppelin, Yes and other British outfits concentrating principally on the US market had melted into Atlantic's caress too. In a stronger position to call shots than they, the Stones were granted their own subsidiary label, Rolling Stones Records, and the appointment of Marshall Chess – son of Leonard, and very much a chip off the old block – as its administrator.

The advance from Atlantic, and the April unleashing of both million-selling 'Brown Sugar' (with 'Bitch' relegated to B-side) and *Sticky Fingers*, came not a moment too soon. The Inland Revenue had marshalled its forces, and, with terrifying sureness, had instigated the closing in of the net, leaving Keith not so much putting a brave face as seeming to deny altogether that his means were by no means infinite.

There was, indeed, no outward sign of impending disaster, very much the opposite as Keith loafed about in incense-smelling complacency between heroin fixes inside 3 Cheyne Walk, made a finger-fluttering entrance to the British charity première of *Performance* and hosted a pre-Christmas party at Olympic Studios. If he ignored the tax bill, perhaps it would go away. It was too huge an amount to take seriously – and so was the mooted and extreme strategy of moving to France at the end of the financial year in April 1971 until the danger had passed. It had even been suggested that there might be more good than harm in the Stones forswearing allegiance to the Queen and becoming naturalised Frenchmen.

Keith flitted fitfully from withdrawn moodiness to conducting himself as if free from all care and responsibility on what was understood by everyone else to be a farewell tour of Britain, commencing in Newcastle and concluding on 26 March 1971 with two televised shows at the Marquee of blessed memory. These dates were marred, or supplemented, by Keith, who, in a foul temper when he arrived, flailed his guitar like a golf club at the head of manager Harold Pendleton, Chad-like at the performers' feet, for reasons traceable to some half-forgotten slight in 1962 when the world was young.

Then it was back to self-imposed house arrest in Cheyne Walk, strumming chords, sinking into a doze in front of the television, smoking, smoking... He'd wander over to the heavily curtained window to peep glumly at the street, wondering if he was under police surveillance from this parked van or that raincoated geezer scanning an *Evening Standard* by the lamppost.

Keith knew, and the Stones organisation knew that he knew, that he was obliged to leave. However, like a pampered puppet emperor of Imperial China whose concubines had to carry him to the commode, he hardly admitted the existence of a world outside his own walls until, devoid of will, he was shepherded into the waiting limousine that was to bear him to Heathrow and a flight of not quite two hours along the air corridor to the Cote D'Azur.

11 An Englishman Abroad

'I can't forget that I am English, but they kicked us out of our own country. We didn't have the sort of money they were asking for, so we left.'

– Keith Richards[1]

If flushed out of England with bad grace, Keith was prepared to make a go of France. Ensconced in a Cannes hotel, he and Anita were photographed at the local film festival for a screening of *Gimmie Shelter*, and seen inspecting likely looking rentable properties.

They settled with startling decisiveness on 'Nellcote', a Riviera villa of white marble balustrades and high ceilings, overlooking Villefrance-sur-Mer and the blue curvature of the Mediterranean. Further away, the snowcaps of the maritime Alps could be made out, as could the coastal roads to Nice and, in the opposite direction, Monte Carlo.

The Nazis had commandeered the residence after Hitler's rape of France in 1940, and the creation of the collaborationist Vichy government. Another former occupant was a British admiral who authorised the planting of disparate varieties of trees – mainly pine, cypress and palm – and unusual flora in grounds that swept down to the private beach where Keith would swim and sunbathe. He also applied himself to sailing, spending many an afternoon on the rolling waves in his yacht, *Mandrax*, 42 tonnes of wood and steel, over 20 feet long – with only the *phut* of engine and groan of cordage to remind him of modern times on the mainland.

Within weeks, Nellcote had been customised to the new incumbent's specifications, most pragmatically with the installation of recording equipment in the basement of what had been nicknamed 'Keith's Coffee House'. If there was a storm centre of the Stones' operation in exile it was surely Nellcote, where musicians and payroll courtiers conferred, journalists were turned away, freeloaders sponged, telephones rang from Los Angeles, London and New York, and Richards greeted callers, among them Gram Parsons and Bobby Keyes, whose drawling ebullience was more comfortable than the stilted 'Franglais' of the socialites he hardly troubled to get to know, choosing as he did eventually to shun evening meals in restaurants frequented by both tanned 'beautiful people' and expatriate gentlefolk nearing retirement age.

Instead, like a mediaeval baron, Keith would preside over up to 50 daily dinner guests at Nellcote. Waking up, he'd almost expect to yawn and stretch to the reading of minutes or starstruck drivellings, so constant was the flux of visitors – some more intrusive than others. 'Keith had this entourage of hangers-on, who were always around the house,' groaned Anita, 'There was no private life, no time to talk.'[2]

Among compensations was that, free from the financial overheads of a hired studio, the electronic den below stairs enabled Richards to potter about with sound, tape the wackiest demos and begin a day's recording with nothing prepared. While mixing and mastering was to take place in more sophisticated locations in the USA, every note of the Stones' only non-compilation double album, *Exile On Main Street*,[3] was to be hand-tooled at Nellcote[4] over 1971's blazing Cote D'Azur summer into its autumn, when heavy air flopped over the place like a wet raincoat.

'Keith works on his own emotional rhythm pattern,' smiled engineer Glyn Johns, summoned from Surrey. 'If he thinks it's necessary to spend three hours working on a riff, he'll do it while everyone else picks their nose. I've never seen him stop and explain something.'[1]

Grasping the reins of what he called 'Stones Mach II', Richards had never been out on a longer limb, particularly as Mick was absenting himself from sessions during the initial lovestruck months of his marriage to the first Mrs Jagger. This was regrettable but far from disastrous as Keith took more or less sole charge with not so much bossy hauteur as a laconic obstinacy. 'If things don't suit Keith, he won't go along with it,' sighed Bill Wyman, 'and that's the end of the subject. When asked why not, Keith would reply, "Because I don't want to".'[1]

Nonchalant proficiency deferred to the spirit of the moment and a home-made passion, enhanced by Keith's increasingly more eccentric rhythmic shifts and the very surroundings in which, as more and more musical trimmings were discarded, direction and outcome shone through with the same sepia-tinted clarity as the discs' packaging. In this respect, Keith's hard listening to the *in situ* incantations of pre-war bluesmen, taped in the mediaeval period of recording technology, hadn't been wasted – particularly those of Robert Johnson: 'He was playing with rooms,' concluded Keith, 'I think that he was very, very aware of sound and a room, and where the sound of his guitar would bounce off the corner. He was into ambience.'[5]

Like *Don Quixote*, the novel on which Cervantes' reputation will always rest, *Exile On Main Street* – Keith's baby, conceived in Nellcote's cellar – became the yardstick by which future Rolling Stones output would be measured. It was to be – with *Sgt Pepper* and The Beach Boys' *Pet Sounds* – near the top of those 'Hundred Greatest Albums' polls that rear up periodically in the media. Yet there would be a profound lack of retrospective honesty about *Exile On Main Street* – which wasn't appreciated especially greatly in the season of its release. It certainly wasn't regarded as the classic that today's younger pop journalists have been raised to think it is.

While it crept to Number One in the USA, it had been disparaged by *Rolling Stone* with 'too much of *Exile* is simply forgettable'.[6] Adding injury to insult, it finished just outside the Top 30 in *Billboard*'s bestselling LPs of 1972 list – and among higher placings was *Hot Rocks 1964–1971*, an anthology of pre-Atlantic Stones material, which had spread itself thinly enough to sell more copies without rising above Number Four.

As to who was responsible for *Hot Rocks* – and then 1972's *More Hot Rocks (Big Hits And Fazed Cookies)* – there was no serious doubt, though hearsay that Allen Klein had also delayed the release of *Exile On Main Street* with a court injunction proved unfounded. Once a hero who'd bullied Decca into parting with an eye-stretching advance royalty cheque back in 1965, Klein was now a villain of the darkest hue. Auditors appointed by the Stones had uncovered enough evidence of 'mismanagement of funds' from his mazy balance sheets to justify a multi-million dollar lawsuit. Almost as an afterthought, there was an action against Andrew Oldham and Eric Easton too for 'royalty deprivation'. Counter-suits and further mud-slinging ensured that it would take years for the blizzards of writs to subside into complicated but fixed channels whereby the assorted and incoming monies could be divided and sent to the sometimes disgruntled parties, a process summarised by Richards as 'the price of an education'.[7]

Keith's eyes would glaze over during the most tenacious discussions about Stones finance. More urgent a worry during his stay at Nellcote, however, was a charge of assault emanating from a 'road rage' incident in May with an Italian tourist, but when it came to court just before Christmas, the bench accepted Richards' plea of self-defence. The following year, a scuffle with a pair of photographers in one fog-bound airport led to similar months of groping for reasons why it would or would not be pursued before nothing more was heard from them or their regional justiciary.

By then, Richards was becoming oblivious to the

consequences of behaviour that anticipated the unmannerly conceits of punk by half a decade. Another precedent was being forged by The New York Dolls, Rolling Stones lookalikes working in the Big Apple's *demimonde* clubland who issued an eponymous 1972 debut album that was an accurate encapsulation of a familiar, if excitingly slipshod, stage act. This was built round 'Personality Crisis', 'Looking For A Kiss' and other compositions that were reflective of a hard-living corporate lifestyle characterised by alcoholism, drug overdoses and an anti-everything stance that was reminiscent of the Stones' 1960s excesses while being cited later as nascent punk. It is, perhaps, significant that, on their last legs, the Dolls were managed by future Sex Pistols Svengali Malcolm McLaren. Provocative ploys (such as projecting them as communists) could not, however, stay the decline of these titans of trash.

'It'd be better if they had their own thing entirely,' commented Keith, 'I'm sure they'd be happier if they were making it on the strength of something a little less tenuous than having a guy in the band who happens to look like somebody that's rather more famous.'[8]

Richards was equally bemused by the recent antics of Chuck Berry. While mixing work with pleasure when putting the final touches to *Exile On Main Street*, Richards dared to trespass onto the boards to barré the over-familiar chord changes for three numbers during an ill-humoured performance by his boyhood hero at the Hollywood Palladium. Emptying his lungs with a *whoosh* afterwards, he was to gloom later, 'God, you look at some of these old rock 'n' rollers. Experience counts as a hindrance more than a help. Look at Chuck Berry now. I laugh down my sleeve that the guy ever turned me on. How can somebody that epitomised the whole thing by consistently making great rock 'n' roll records, sound like that.'[8]

Keith was referring specifically to Berry's 'My Ding-A-Ling', a descent into lavatorial humour that topped the 1972 charts in both Britain and the USA for a respective month and fortnight. 'He's always pulled that sort of novelty song bit out at certain junctures in his career,' explained Keith as much to himself as anyone else, 'and, yeah, it's feeble, but still he is trying to inject a certain amount of humour into rock, and God knows it needs it right now.'[1]

That was certainly the case in the States where, while James Taylor was going off the boil, 'progressive' FM radio was most receptive to the unchallenging likes of Johnny Winter, Humble Pie, Elton John, The Climax Blues Band and, especially, The Eagles,[9] whose stock-in-trade was country-rock of a type pioneered by Gram Parsons, only much more soporific. One such station, KDAY in Los Angeles, spun two illicitly acquired *Exile On Main Street* tracks non-stop for the best part of a day during the build-up to the coast-to-coast barnstormer by 'the biggest draw in the history of mankind',[10] according to Bill Graham, perhaps the most influential promoter on the circuit.

Graham had been sickened by the Stones' conduct during the Altamont tour, and had had no qualms about saying so, but it seemed that all that was excused. *Exile On Main Street*'s spin-off 45s – 'Tumbling Dice' and, with a convincing lead vocal from Keith, 'Happy' – were either hovering or about to hover around the middle of the US Top 30. Also, an attendance of 30,000 at a performance in Canada was not unusual – and neither were the riots, the police cordons, the forged tickets, the death threats and the showbiz 'personalities' falling over themselves to have their pictures taken with Mick Jagger.

'The newspapers aren't as interested in me,' shrugged Keith, 'All you hear about me is when the warrants are out.'[11] An abiding image of the Stones on the road in the early 1970s is a snapshot taken at a customs area of a seated Richards in deep slumber beneath a notice pleading for patience because 'A Drug Free America Comes First!'

His stimulant-ravaged personal history was so widely known that an amused cheer from the sea of leather, denim and hair would well up to his swigging of a bottle of Jack Daniels or Southern Comfort between numbers. Purportedly, there were also lines of cocaine and heroin on top of his amplifier, but less conspicuous were the 'DCs' – 'dirty cigarettes' – containing heroin that he smoked while just about keeping a grip on the music for the duration of the show.

Drugs were such common currency in rock circles at this point that a story went the rounds of a ten per cent budget requirement, attributed to 'miscellaneous', for a US trek by The Pretty Things – whose Phil May is credited with the dubious honour of originating the euphemism 'Charlie' — restricted code for cocaine. 'It was a way of writing off expenses,' he elucidated, 'so I invented a fictitious road manager worth three hundred dollars a week.'

Messing about with narcotics had lead to death for a real member of the Things' road crew. Thanks to heroin, US singer Janis Joplin had already given to fish and the air that which she had refused to men when her ashes were shed on the Pacific just over a week after her passing – with a needle sticking out of her left arm – in October 1970. Moreover, the same destructive tastes and co-related bouts of suicidal depression had resulted in long lay-offs and a fall in quality of successive albums for Johnny Winter – to the extent that his backing combo offered their services to his steadier younger brother, Edgar.

If not yet nursing serious debilities, Keith Richards too was heading for an abyss in which 'junk takes the place of everything. You don't need a chick, you don't need music, you don't need nothing. It doesn't get you anywhere. It's not called junk for nothing.' [12]

There weren't any ill-effects that he felt he couldn't handle then. Anita too seemed to be coping after she and Keith had undergone a failed attempt at weaning themselves off heroin in a clinic in Middlesex before the evacuation to France. On re-encountering the outside world, they were exposed almost immediately to their 'trigger points': the places, people and circumstances conducive to relapses. 'Twenty-four hours after we occupied the villa, we were back injecting ourselves,' confessed Anita, 'because a cure's no good when you live in the middle of pushers and users. God knows there were plenty of both on the Riviera.'[2]

A second pregnancy prompted Anita to seek residential treatment in Geneva, over the Swiss border, and she'd been 'clean', however temporarily, for four months when a sister for Marlon – named Dandelion after the 1967 single – was prised into the world on 17 April 1972.

Switzerland proved so agreeable that the family moved to Montreux on the facing bank of Lake Geneva in August. It was also a bolt hole from the unwelcome interest that the Riviera *gendarmerie* had in pop groups living on its beat. Posing as drug dealers, diligent investigators penetrated the Stones' inner circle, and uncovered enough malpractice for warrants to be issued in December against Richards, Pallenberg and a third party – which may have been either Bobby Keyes or Nellcote's overworked cook – though 'the first I heard of my arrest was when I read it in the newspaper one morning,' recalled Keith.[10]

This new revelation perturbed Doris Richards more than it did her son. Her chief concern was the welfare of Dandelion. 'Doris thought I wasn't fit to look after her,' opined Anita, 'which I probably wasn't by then.'[13] Resuming her habit quite openly while the child was still in nappies, she was no longer denying that her dependency was critical, 'I was more interested in getting my supply than looking after the kids. Instead of getting them dinner, I'd go out and wander around, meeting people, and spending the night looking for UFOs. When Keith was away, I'd be starting to get off the heroin, really trying, but then he'd return, and I'd be on it as bad as ever.'[2]

12 The Addicted Man

'I don't know if I've been extremely lucky or if it's that subconscious careful, but I've never turned blue in somebody else's bathroom. I consider that the height of bad manners.'

– Keith Richards[1]

Bob Dylan's inauguration as an *ex officio* don of Princeton University in 1970 had been a sign that academia had ceased distancing itself from pop – which was soon to begin its infiltration of school curricula. It was remarkable that, unlike film, jazz and other disciplines pertaining to the Coca-Cola century just gone, it had taken until then for higher education to take seriously music that has been recorded for the masses since before the death of Victoria.

In 1973's summer term, California State University inaugurated a degree course in 'rock studies' – and Keith Richards was the subject of at least one thesis. So began a long journey to some sort of universally recognised respectability for Keith, who was then fresh from sessions for the Stones' next album, *Goat's Head Soup*, at Dynamic Sound Studios in Kingston, the capital of Jamaica. It was to be mixed at Island Studios, which, if located in London, were owned by Chris Blackwell, Kingston born and bred. The flagship act of his record label – also called Island – was Traffic, who were recording in Jamaica at the same time as the Stones. As well as being a pleasant escape from that wet British winter, the Commonwealth republic was favoured by Traffic's Steve Winwood because, 'Jamaican music is itself particularly English and African for obvious historical reasons, and that's what attracted me to it.'[2]

Such hands-on endorsement by Traffic and the Stones, fully integrated mainstays of rock's ruling class, indicated correctly that West Indian sounds were no longer an alien commodity – 'skinhead music' – to the general pop market. Starring Montego Bay ska exponent Jimmy Cliff as a Jamaican gunman, the film *The Harder They Come* had been on in a cinema near you in 1972, and had been patronised by white sixth formers and undergraduates – who also bought its soundtrack album.

Via the auspices of Cliff and mainstream acceptance of Bob Marley And The Wailers – and, to a smaller extent, the likes of Ijahman, Toots And The Maytals, Burning Spear and Sly And The Revolutionaries – reggae in the 1970s would outflank even blues as the new 'twisted voice of the underdog' and student disco accessory, and its stars' names were dropped in hip circles. Marley reminded George Harrison 'so much of Dylan' – and as for his rhythm, 'it's so simple and yet so beautiful'.[3] One of Eric Clapton's bestselling singles would be a version of Marley's 'I Shot The Sheriff', while Cat Stevens – a 1960s pop star who had re-emerged as a post-Woodstock singer-songwriter – penned Jimmy Cliff's 1970 UK smash, 'Wild World'. Cat's own jerky 'Can't Keep It In' in 1972 had been his idea of reggae, just as a solo Paul Simon had been that same year with 'Mother And Child Reunion', actually recorded in the West Indies with local musicians.

Most germane to this discussion is that, while Traffic worked on their *Shoot Out At The Fantasy Factory* album at Strawberry Hill Studios in Kingston, and the Stones on *Goat's Head Soup* in Dynamic Sound, Keith Richards fell in love with Jamaica and its culture, going so far as to purchase what amounted to an official residence in December 1972 at Point of View in Ocho Rios, an upmarket settlement worlds away from Kingston's poorest suburb, Trench Town. However, it was such ghettos that spawned the brash, confident domestic pop acceptable to non-plebeian, even intellectual, Caucasians. Contrasting with 'My Boy Lollipop' like the Moon to the Earth, this expressed a swelling anger and proclaimed that a change was gonna come.

As well as being enraptured by the music and attitude, Keith liked the actuality as much as the idea of fraternising with those artists who had emerged from Trench Town – in particular, Peter Tosh, Marley's musical lieutenant until 1975. Like the other Wailers, Tosh and Marley were dope-smoking Rastafarians, a religious sect that Chris Blackwell had always understood to be 'killers, anti-white'⁴ until his motorboat struck a reef and sank along the desolate Hellshire coastline near Spanish Town.

He swam to shore and, hours later, approached a hut miles along the lonely beach. When six dreadlocked Rastas emerged, Blackwell almost fainted with shock. However, instead of being tortured to death, he enjoyed frugal hospitality of seafood, Bible readings and back-to-Africa sermons pertinent to worship of living god Haile Selassie, lately deposed emperor of Ethiopia, who was known as 'The Lion of Judah'. As well as perhaps reminding him vaguely of his adolescent years in Harrow, Greater London's most exclusive public school for boys, the encounter led Blackwell to sympathy in place of ingrained fear for Jamaica's most shunned sub-culture.

The less sheltered instincts of Keith's upbringing facilitated an easier integration into Rasta society when he started hanging around with Tosh and his cronies in the 'sound system' dives of downtown Kingston, where tinnitis-inducing volume effused from gigantic speakers. When removed from unintelligible platitudes shouted over the racket, Keith spoke of producing Rastafarian acts for Rolling Stones Records in between drawing on spliffs laced with 'ganja' – marijuana – that were provided by his new pals.

Ganja may have helped sustain Tosh's and Marley's spiritual resolve, but Linda Ronstadt (a singer-songwriter type – except she didn't write many songs), would brag that, 'I can sing better after shooting smack in both my arms than after eating too much.'[5] Yet the mid-1970s brought strong hostility to illicit drugs from many musicians, both in interview and record grooves. 'The general consensus of opinion is that it's impossible to do anything creative unless you use chemicals,' snarled Frank Zappa,[5] whose 'Cocaine Decisions' swiped at the stimulant most prevalent in the music industry in the 1970s and 1980s, apart from alcohol, while John Mayall's 'Accidental Suicide' was less a tribute to the late Jimi Hendrix than a cautionary tale of the same kidney as Steppenwolf's 'The Pusher' (whose trade created addicts 'with tombstones in their eyes'), 1971's 'Behind Blue Eyes' by The Who and Eric Clapton's 'Cocaine'.

Even The Grateful Dead, confrères of The Merry Pranksters, had wagged a rebuking finger in 'Casey Jones' with its 'you'd better watch you speed' hookline – and Godfather of Soul James Brown exerted his quasi-monarchical influence to block trafficking in black areas with 1972's admonitory 'King Heroin', a graceful but hard-hitting rap before the form evolved into an excuse for gross *braggadocio*. Born of a dream, Brown's recitation over an unobtrusive riff lists the unsavoury aspects of addiction, how it can 'put a gun in your hand and make you a killer' and 'make the most virile of men forget their sex', before signing off with 'the white horse of heroin will ride you to hell until you are dead, dead, dead' (agonised scream on fade-out).

It was not a warning that Brown himself heeded as he was to be sentenced to six years imprisonment in 1988 on counts that included possession of dangerous drugs. That artificial energy continued to drive pop's foremost icons might be demonstrated too in an ailing Elvis Presley's in-concert 'laughing' version of 'Are You Lonesome Tonight' – and Alice Cooper was to use his sojourn in a drying-out clinic as the theme for a comeback album, *From The Inside*, follow-up to 1977's *Lace And Whisky*. Likewise, 'Maybe I'll get a song out of it,'[1] would be Keith

Richards' reaction to one of the drugs charges that were marking his journey through the decade.[6]

It was becoming a vicious circle. During intervals between this arrest and that court hearing, the very substances at the heart of the matter – notably heroin – would work their short-lived magic, staying the phantoms of paranoia and nudging away from the forefront of his thoughts an obsessive snowballing of a damning case against himself.

Other personal desolations were numbed by heroin too. There'd been another fatality as sudden and, to Keith, more saddening than that of Brian Jones – 'because of the loss of potential, and because he was a good mate'.[7] In Room Eight of the Joshua Tree Inn in Southern California on 19 September 1973, Gram Parsons was celebrating the release of a new album, *Grievous Angel*. To show what a hell of a fellow he was, he washed down morphine tablets with an injudicious quantity of tequila. 'Gram thought he had Keith's metabolism,' groaned Phil Kaufman, 'Keith could eat nails and piss rust. Gram thought he had the same gift.'[8]

Heroin and cocaine present in Parsons' bloodstream already also assisted the promotion of a blackout of such depth that he never came round. That wasn't all. A week later, Kaufman hijacked the coffin and consigned it to flames at the Joshua Tree National Monument further into the San Bernardino desert. This, he explained, was how Gram would have wanted it.[9]

'With discipline and focus, he would have turned into an incredible writer, singer and performer,' grimaced fellow Flying Burrito Brother Chris Hillman, 'He had the talent and the charisma: all the things that were God-given to him – and he threw them away.'[10] Yet, according to Richards, Parsons was making commendable attempts to conquer a dependency on heroin: 'he'd cleaned up, and that was the reason he died. He was recuperating out there, but he got seduced one more time.

He was clean and took a strong shot. It's the one mistake you don't want to make.'[11]

Physician, heal thyself! As well as being involved in talk – albeit, only talk – of marketing a Rolling Stones brand of beer, Richards was emptying even more daily bottles of harder stuff, a crutch that seemed to bring him up to par beneath the proscenium. 'It would be very strange to see Keith Richards on top form without the company of a good tequila,' laughed road manager Peter Rudge.[12] This was a consideration when record entrepreneur Richard Branson invited Keith for an overnight tour of inspection of his new Manor Studios some 20 miles northwest of Oxford. Knowing his guest's predilections, Branson ordered the placing of a bottle of a preferred strong tipple with a discreet napkin over it on a side-table in the master bedroom.

Keith, however, needed more than booze. Otherwise, it's possible that he'd never have tottered onto the stage on many occasions. If he wasn't giggling drunk, he'd be on another planet. By his own graphic admission, he'd metamorphosed into 'a human chemical laboratory, almost like trying to commit suicide without any intention to do it – that stupid, stupid kind of suicide.'[7]

Richards looked the part, especially after his teeth began to rot, and he took to wearing make-up when keeping pace with the glam-rock boom in Britain (that was but a trace element in the US *Hot 100*). Hollow eyes were framed by purple-black blotches that remained even after he had cold-creamed away mascara that had trickled and dried. His emaciation and the corpse-grey colour that he radiated too were exacerbated by an accumulation of fatigue through staying awake for hyperactive days on end, once managing, allegedly, a giddying nine without so much as a catnap.

Gazing in a mirror, he saw ill health, but his mind wandered to other topics the moment he turned away. As well as an indifference to his own welfare, Richards cared little too about

Wee Willie Winkie's apoplexy whenever performances started up to five hours late, as they frequently did these days, owing to Keith keeping both musicians and audience waiting, a 'laid-back' habit that Watts and Jagger in particular found annoying. Lurching from stadium to stadium and conducting himself as if a participant in a heavily subsidised travelling debauch, Richards was frequently missing minutes before the scheduled showtime. Flanked by retainers, he'd then retreat into a dressing room where, from slight therapeutic tipsiness, he might become semi-comatose with further pills, powders, fluids and resins. Always, he made it onto the boards eventually, and, like chronic alcoholic Dylan Thomas pulling himself together for the duration of a poetry reading, Keith's mixture of stimulant intake and work walked a tightrope between straggling indiscipline and near-magical inspiration. Once, his eyelids dropped, his chin sagged onto his chest and he drifted into a gentle snore during a slow ballad, his string-licking plectrum on automatic. Conversely, he'd recollect proudly that 'I played on stage in Australia on acid – in '72 or '73. It was one of the best shows I ever played.'[13]

For much of the time offstage too, he remained several degrees short of being totally 'gone', though when or if he was alone, his drug consumption might have manifested itself in ringing headaches, indigestion, nausea, irritability and other milder repercussions. These may have been apparent to immediate family such as Marlon for whom 'heroin was just something that Dad did', admitted Keith. 'He used to be my roadie when he was five and six and seven. He's seen everything.'[13]

There may have been scarier side-effects such as uncontrollable shivering, convulsive fits and nightmare hallucinations. Stray paragraphs in tabloid newspapers hinted that Richards was taking occasional steps to shake off heroin under supervision – though to do so required decoy tactics and secret destinations as much as spare underwear. Without these precautions, today's private hospital would turn into tomorrow's sea of faces and camera lenses outside the building. Indeed, a couple of 'creative' scribes tried to disguise themselves as staff to get some sordid scoop after a tip-off that Keith was being treated in Harrow's Bowden House, a clinic for the rich and famous where he was supposed to be enduring 'three days of climbing up the walls, then you start to feel better'.[14] He was also purported to be undergoing snake-venom therapy at an institute in Miami, but it transpired that the 'Richards' concerned was a mere relation suffering from a complaint unrelated to drug abuse.

In the music press, the smart money was on Keith in a morbid sweepstake about the next live-fast-die-young pop idol to follow Brian Jones, Jimi Hendrix, Janis Joplin, Jim Morrison of The Doors and like unfortunates to the grave – with the *New Musical Express* nominating him 'The World's Most Elegantly Wasted Human Being'[15]. Moreover, the lyricist of The Righteous Brothers' 1974 US smash, 'Rock 'N' Roll Heaven' – where 'they got one hell of a band' – may have been searching for rhymes for 'Keith' and 'Richards' for the periodically updated concert rendition. The number was already glutinous with both orchestration and declamations with buoyant pride of the names of 'Janis', 'Jimi', 'Jim' and suchlike. Neither of the two unrelated siblings admitted in song that it was the sex-and-drugs-and-rock 'n' roll lifestyle that had led to many of the heroes' wretched ends.

Neither did the Brothers ever get round to mentioning Keith Richards,[16] who 'always gave a wry smile to find out I was Number One on the death list – because, knowing myself, I never considered I was actually pushing it anywhere near the danger limit, although later on, I realised that I was probably a lot closer than I ever admitted – but it kept my feet on the ground, nearly underground, in fact.'[1]

As such, Richards had become by the mid-1970s the Stones' biggest asset and biggest liability. Whereas a 1973 bootleg bearing the title *Keith Richard And His Rolling Stones* emphasised his artistic pre-eminence,[17] he was still holding up proceedings in both auditorium and studio with his muzzy and lackadaisical attitude to timekeeping; a fire in his suite at Hyde Park Corner's Londonderry House Hotel – perhaps caused by smoking half-asleep in bed or a table lamp falling over – had tarred the other Stones with the same brush, and the group had been unable to play in France until after Keith's fine and suspended sentence in autumn 1973 put a full stop to the police raid on Nellcote.

Keith was incorrigible, those around him muttered with vexation rather than humour now. A more recent bust – at 3 Cheyne Walk on 26 June 1973 – had uncovered cannabis, *Chinese* heroin and Mandrax plus a revolver, a shotgun and ammunition. A plea that these had been left there by others when he and Anita were overseas was not accepted at Marlborough Street Magistrates four months later, resulting in a fine for Richards and a conditional discharge for Pallenberg.

That same summer, a rumour had gone the rounds that Keith's condition and correlated reliability had deteriorated so much that he was either intending to leave the Stones or that there'd been an ultimatum disguised as a friendly suggestion that he ought to take a sabbatical to sweat out his, and, by implication, his colleagues', major problem.

13 The Zigzag Wanderer

'It's a drag not to be able to see my Mum just because of
some stupid tax law.'

– Keith Richards[1]

On 31 June 1973, a stray shard of flame ignited Redlands.
Though costly musical equipment and antique furniture were
saved, hosing by the West Sussex fire brigade wasn't enough to
stop profound damage by the spreading inferno. While the moat
was still alive with the brightness of the blaze, Keith Richards
saw ahead of him the months, possibly years, of repair that
would necessitate the property being an uninhabitable no-man's-
land of rubble, planks and tea-drinking artisans.

The long wait for Redlands to be restored to its former
glory combined with Scotland Yard's perceived stakeout of
Cheyne Walk and the mere 90 days per annum in the UK
permitted to tax exiles began to unfetter the gypsy in Keith's
soul. With Peter Tosh, apparently, all but squatting in Point of
View, and Anita's imminent deportation from Jamaica – the
aftermath of an arrest that had climaxed an evening out with
some Rastas – there was no permanent base outside England
so, with a mountain of keepsakes and memorabilia in storage
in a Brooklyn warehouse, and with Pallenberg at his side, Keith
Richards roamed from hotel to expensive hotel – where he'd be
conducted to the best seat in the restaurant and the
switchboard or room service would relay complimentary
tickets and social invitations, offering flattery without

friendship to one whose every action was worth half a page in *The Sun* or *The Los Angeles Times*.

At the reception desk, his newly inserted earring – an outrageous male adornment at the time – silver skull signet ring and general picaresque demeanour drew muffled titters from those to whom opulence had always been second nature. After checking out, if he wasn't on an aeroplane, he'd be in the departure lounge, waiting for the next one, jetting from, say, Paris to New York with the ease of a daily commuter on the 8.22 to Waterloo.

During a relatively lengthy stay in Switzerland in 1974, a blithe fatalism had him mingling among shoppers in a Montreux precinct; sipping a quiet *Stein* in a Zurich beer garden or taking the air in the Alpine foothills. Yet, if unmolested by autograph hunters and worse, his advice as a Grand Old Man of pop was sought by affluent young locals who wanted to follow in his footsteps: 'They come up to me in the street and say, "I'm in a band. How do we get to be really big?" – and I say, "Well, look, why don't you try starving?" They can't comprehend that, they're so rich.'[1]

Keith's life of suitcases would take him to Rotterdam in the New Year for recording dates that also served as auditions for a guitarist to supersede Mick Taylor, who had never felt as if he quite belonged. Among those under consideration for the post were Steve Marriott, weary of a shallow megastardom accrued over 22 US tours with Humble Pie, the 'supergroup' he'd formed after the sundering of his Small Faces. Just before Christmas, he and Keith had been thrown together as guitarists on the sloweddown revival of 'Get Off Of My Cloud', which was the title song of a new Alexis Korner album.[2]

Present on other tracks, Marriott's Humble Pie cohort Peter Frampton was another possibility. Oiling the wheels would be his intended inclusion of an overhaul of 'Jumpin' Jack Flash' on the album that was the small beginning of solo success for him in North America later in the decade. The composing royalties from this were to provide – so Richards was to inform Frampton

– the exact amount required for the purchase of a desired house in South Salem, near Westchester in upstate New York.

Debating the Stones' future too, the press put forward Eric Clapton, then at a vocational loose end, for the job as well as Rory Gallagher, former leader of the highly rated 'power trio' Taste; Mick Ronson, late of David Bowie's Spiders From Mars; ex-Battered Ornament Chris Spedding, respected studio shellback and one-hit-wonder with 1975's 'Motorbikin'', and Wilko Johnson, as renowned for his spasmodic movements onstage as his picking with Dr Feelgood, a busy R&B outfit from Essex. What was Dick Taylor doing these days? The search fanned out to the USA, boiling down to Harvey Mandel from Canned Heat and Wayne Perkins, a Texan who'd given a Bob Marley album, *Catch A Fire*, a hard rock touch up.

There was substance in some of the speculations. For a while, Perkins seemed the clear favourite, 'but he was American, and we had to own up we were an English band,' concluded Richards. [3] As English as Perkins wasn't, Jeff Beck too was heard in Rotterdam – on a remaindered instrumental arrangement of Martha And The Vandellas' 'Heatwave' – but resisted overtures to pledge himself to the Stones because, 'I was used to conceiving a notion, putting it on tape, and having it finished by the evening. They had trouble turning up at the same time.' [4]

Not so pernickety about the Stones' inconsistent, ragged methodology, Ron Wood, Beck's sometime bass player, had, with singer Rod Stewart, joined forces with what remained of The Small Faces after Marriott's departure in 1969. With no attributive adjective now, The Faces had, after a sluggish start, emerged as one of the most popular concert attractions of the early 1970s, but were going off the boil as a chart act, owing in part to the greater success of Stewart's parallel solo career. Another crack appeared when Wood was in the process of recording 1974's *I've Got My Own Album To Do*, a venture that was noteworthy for its big-name sleeve credits – with

Keith Richards conspicuous on guitar, keyboards and backing vocals. It was through Keith that Ron reworked 'If You Gotta Make A Fool Of Somebody', the Freddie And The Dreamers smash from 1963.[5]

Almost as a matter of course, Richards pitched in when, on 14 June 1974, Wood promoted his LP with an all-star line-up accompanying him at Kilburn's Gaumont State Theatre, a further indication that the end was nigh for The Faces. However, the final disencumberance to Ron becoming a temporary and then full-time Rolling Stone was that most of a Stones single, 'It's Only Rock 'N' Roll' – one of several mid-1970s chart-busters with 'rock 'n' roll' in the title[6] – was realised in Wood's home studio in Richmond, though its production was attributed to 'The Glimmer Twins', a freshly concocted pseudonym for Richards and Jagger.

Ron could never hope to penetrate Keith and Mick's caste-within-a-caste, but, during the making of *I've Got My Own Album To Do*, a restricted code evolved quickly between Richards and himself to the degree that utterances unamusing to anybody else would have them howling with laughter when ostensibly cudgelling an unshaven objectivity on a mix of 'If You Gotta Make A Fool Of Somebody' as milk floats braved the dawn chill. In the way that close friends revile each other affectionately, Ron would describe Keith as 'a filthy swine. We're like naughty schoolboys. You'll never take that away from us.'[7]

Musically, however, the crux of the Stones was not the interplay between the guitarists but that between Richards and Watts. In the words of drummer Alan Barwise, a local legend in Reading, Berkshire, 'When Keith and Charlie knit together – a combination of economy and drive – what the rest of the band does doesn't really matter.' Nevertheless, Richards and Wood's liaison was closer to the former's fretboard concord with Brian Jones than the more pronounced lead-rhythm division with Mick Taylor. 'Both Ron and Keith are brilliant rhythm guitarists,' exclaimed Mick Jagger, 'It allows a certain cross-trading of riffs not previously possible.'[8] It was there for all to hear on a jaunt round the USA in 1975 by a Stones that was, beamed Keith, 'less slick and sophisticated sounding than the other one at its best when everyone was in tune and could hear each other. This is a lot dirtier and rougher, and a lot more exciting.'[8]

A certain extra-tonal piquancy emanated from Keith's guitar, which had been customised to possess just *five* machine-heads. The new instrument also contained one of the properties of a banjo (and a sitar) – a vibrating 'sympathetic' string that, so Keith observed, 'got some kind of drone going. Ordinarily, when you change chords, the previous chord is completely dead.'[3]

Further preparations for the trip included Richards' acquisition of a Bob Marley T-shirt to wear onstage, and urgent and extensive dental treatment in a Swiss surgery. Between stiff-upper-lip sessions under the drill, he taped some demos in a local studio, and visited a residential drugs clinic in Geneva, an appointment that gave rise to a myth that Keith had crossed the Alps to exchange his entire quota of drug-polluted blood for a transfusion of eight efficaciously clean pints.

During the tour, he'd grin askance at such tales, and crack gruesome one-liners like 'I only ever get ill when I give up drugs',[8] but now and then a shadow of unspeakable misery would cross his face. Apparently, as well as the doctors in Switzerland shaking their heads over the obvious diagnosis – that his present organic deterioration and arterial blockage was the legacy of heroin *et al* – they'd warned that unless he mended his ways immediately, he could be dead within six months.

Frightened, he made at least a token attempt to abstain from his usual behaviour. Yet the prescribed regime of avoiding stress and living a quiet life for a while sat ill with situations that were an avenue for unholier-than-thou roisterings; having to assiduously veto Jagger's plan for a Grand Entrance on a cavalcade of elephants for the Seattle show, and being the cynosure of spotlights and tens of thousands of eyes as amorphous as frogspawn, especially when Mick brought him forward to give 'em 'Happy'. This he did with a husky vehemence dredged from a throat with vocal cords beyond remedy through him tearing the cellophane off up to five daily packets of cigarettes since adolescence.

Keith's constitution wasn't improved either during off-duty hours that weren't allowed to pass without incident. A stolen afternoon driving in the Arkansas lowlands with Ron Wood and road manager Jim Callaghan was blighted when the Highway Patrol burst from a lay-by and flagged down the vehicle after its tyres spun on loose gravel when pulling up outside a restaurant in a town called Fordyce. In the Deep South, disapproval of men with long hair was still expressed by actions beyond simply some Oscar Wilde yelling 'Get yer 'air cut!' from a passing car. The cops, crew cut and belligerently masculine, were determined, therefore, to make something of it.

Though riled by Callaghan and Wood's soft-sounding English accents too, their prime target was the instantly recognisable Richards – though they weren't sure whether it had been him or Jim who'd been responsible for 'reckless driving'. How about illegal possession of an offensive weapon, to wit a penknife complete with bottle opener and device for winkling pebbles from horses' hooves?

It was a funny story to tell the others when work resumed the next day at the Cotton Bowl in Dallas. After much heart-searching, Bob Marley And The Wailers had spurned an offer – with Keith their principal champion – to support the Stones, preferring to headline a concurrent US tour in their own right. Both acts chanced to be performing in Los Angeles on the same July night, but an enthralled Stones deputation found the time to attend a Marley matinée at the city's Roxy Theatre.

The most practical recent evidence of the British group's captivation with contemporary reggae, however, had been the imposition of *moderato* rhythms straight from a Kingston sound-system dancehall onto 'Luxury' from *It's Only Rock 'N' Roll* and 'Cherry Oh Baby' on 1976's *Black And Blue*, the album that Richards would dismiss with 'rehearsing guitar players, that's what that one was about.'[9]

Some exploratory sessions for a mooted follow-up took place at the Manor where the group enjoyed the swimming pool, snooker den and other facilities that were more agreeable than any in certain urban complexes they could name. How more civilised it was also to be served deferential meals washed down with home-brewed ale at the huge oak table in the cloistered Manor's ancient hall with its stained glass, crossed swords and exposed beams.

This block-booked week was marked less by its aural results than Richard Branson watching, with fascination, Keith Richards' fireside masterclass in rolling a Jamaican-style reefer – and the arrival of a burly West Indian waving a pistol and demanding an audience with Richards – who, he shouted, was in the throes of a liaison with his wife. That this accusation was founded in fact became manifest when, from the rumpled disorder of a night of passion, Keith and the lady concerned bolted out of a sidedoor and across a lawn towards the undergrowth that shrouded a reach of the Thames. As neither were adept at dressing while running, they were quite naked, but there was nothing for it but to hail a punt full of blazered and straw-boatered university students, and be rowed to embarrassed safety before the betrayed husband – who'd leapt into his ticking-over car and turned an enraged steering wheel in their direction – was able to head them off.

Now an old friend who used to be a lover, Anita clung to her dignity as the official bedmate and mother of his children, outwardly more amused than angry. 'Keith started to have girlfriends that I found out about,' she shrugged, 'and I started to see other men – but things got better when I had our third child. Keith announced that we were going to be married, and he began to make elaborate wedding plans.'[10]

Richards thought aloud about a wedding onstage during an imminent Stones tour of Europe, but the subject was dropped when, less than three months after his birth, influenza killed the boy they'd named Tara.

'The baby died, and, in a sense, we died too,' believed Anita[10] as Keith, a trouper of 'the show must go on' stamp, insisted that the tragedy be kept from the media, and the remaining dates honoured, beginning with a show that very evening – 4 June 1976 – at the Abattoirs in Paris. When the present round of stupid songs about chicks, only rock 'n' roll and jumpin' Jack Flash being a gas-gas-gas were over a fortnight later in Vienna, it was noticed that he seemed his usual self, except his talk grew steadily louder, his eyes brighter, his carousing more manic during what amounted to a wake for not only Tara but a tired relationship that muddled on because neither partner had enough motivation to finish it.

Without premeditation, death had come close to Keith and Anita – and Marlon – during the British leg of the tour in May when they were motoring in the Bentley through the night from Stafford's New Bingley Hall to London. In the grey of early morning on the fast lane of the M1 near Newport Pagnell service station, driver Keith struck the central reservation barrier. He rode out the subsequent skid across a thankfully empty motorway into grass beyond the hard shoulder.

Surrounded by flashing blue lights, he comforted his passengers while a grim-faced constable jotted down details of the crash before turning his attention to the contents of the known drug miscreant's wrecked vehicle. A silver tube attached to a necklace was discovered. It contained a substance identified later as cocaine. The tax disc on the shattered windscreen was out of date too. Finally, a tab of LSD was found about Keith's person at Newport Pagnell police station.

Before the rest of Britain woke up, Richards was released from custody with an almost certain prospect of another 'guilty' verdict when the case came up. It seemed fanciful to hope for more than the most unsavoury future – and the worst was yet to come, but from this dark hour, the slow pageant of sunrise was already unfolding.

14 The Late Arrival

'What's on trial is the same thing that's always been on trial:
dear old them and us. I find this all a bit weary. I've done my
stint in the dock. Why don't they pick on The Sex Pistols?'
— Keith Richards [1]

As a crusher pummelled Keith's written-off Bentley into a cube,
there was much afoot in 1976 as British pop was preparing once
again to bare its teeth to the world. This had started humbly
enough in and around London taverns and associated clubs with
a movement that one pressured *Melody Maker* newshound
called 'pub-rock'. The phrase stuck after it grew in impetus and
became more cohesive when accompanied by the proliferation of
specialist 'fanzines' and haphazard cells of archivist-performers
like me. Indeed, my first social invitation to my future wife was
to a jumble sale where my heart pounded with anticipation as I
squeezed between hags blocking access to a pile of scratched 45s
on a white elephant stall. You can always get a new girlfriend,
but some of those records might have been really rare.

Yet, however grass-roots its genesis, as pub-rock spread
throughout Britain and Europe, Dr Feelgood, Ace, The Kursaal
Flyers, Ian Dury, Eddie And The Hot Rods and other of its
practitioners were to be swept from the nicotine haze of
Islington's Hope-and-Anchor and the Red Cow in
Hammersmith into the Top 40, and Bees Make Honey landed a
support spot to glam-rock supremos T Rex just as the wind
changed. Moreover, pub-rock's very prehistory had climaxed

with Brinsley Schwarz's attempt in 1970 to start at the top, crippled with nerves at New York's Fillmore auditorium before a plane-load of British music press.

'In the aftermath of, perhaps, the greatest hype in pop history, Brinsley Schwarz would become a symbol for anti-hype,' wrote Will Birch, The Kursaal Flyers' drummer, in *No Sleep Till Canvey Island: The Great Pub Rock Revolution,*[2] a chronicle that transports you to the jovial atmosphere of licenced premises *circa* 1976, where, say, Rocky Sharpe And The Replays, The Count Bishops, Duke Duke and the Dukes or France's roly-poly Little Bob Story are playing with wantonly and thrillingly retrogressive verve, and flicking a V-sign at everything detestable about the stadium superstar alternative and the distancing of the common-or-garden pop group from its essentially teenage audience.

During this, one of the most pivotal eras of UK pop, 'street level' acclaim was also accorded to all manner of resurrected entities from the Swinging Sixties. These ranged from The Troggs to Johnny Kidd's surviving Pirates to the also-ran Rockin' Vickers to The Steve Gibbons Band, derived ultimately from The Ugly's [*sic*], pride of mid-1960s Birmingham. After acquiring a strong reputation on the pub-rock circuit, Gibbons' time would come with a revival of 'Tulane', a Chuck Berry track from 1969. As a 1977 single, Steve's version would shin up the domestic Top 20 – just as The Electric Light Orchestra had done four years earlier with 'Roll Over Beethoven'.[3]

Contradictory and far-fetched rumours abounding about what had happened to Dick Taylor were also centred on pub-rock now that the one about him rejoining the Stones had faded. No, these days, he was a manager for a jeans firm but had demoted himself to van driver to more easily burn the candle at both ends in a pub-rock combo, Auntie And The Men From Uncle. Yes, but wasn't he up there with The Mekons at the Music Machine?

The Downliners Sect – who'd thrown in the towel not long before Dick quit The Pretty Things in 1969 – wondered if there was a place in the pub-rock sun for them too. Indeed, there was and, if some customers remembered wild evenings in Studio 51 with affection, The Sect also amassed a younger following that spilled out onto the pavement when they headlined at the Fulham Greyhound, High Wycombe's Nag's Head and even back at the 100 Club. A resumed recording itinerary had both repackaged 1960s LPs and new releases high up independent charts throughout Europe – and in 1979, the once-and-future cult R&B group delivered what might have been the finest 1960s R&B album of the 1970s, if you follow my drift, in *Showbiz*, a collection ranging from nostalgic 'Richmond Rhythm & Blues' to 'Break Up', one of these worth-the-whole-price-of-the-album excerpts – and a surefire hit if only a Rolling Stones-sized public could have heard it.

Whether pub-rock gave pause for thought for the Stones themselves is another matter. As far as it was tenable, they were at least mulling over the possibilities of returning to roots by playing a couple of low-profile dates in Studio 51-sized clubs in the near future, and maybe issuing the results on an album.

When in London, various Stones had hazarded excursions to see for themselves how pub-rock was catching on. They had become aware too that, festering beneath it, were outfits in artistic debt to one whose stage wardrobe was bespoke by a shop called 'Sex' – formerly 'Let It Rock' – towards the wrong end of King's Road – and equidistant from both Edith Grove and Cheyne Walk. Sex sold garments tailored by Vivienne Westwood, girlfriend of its proprietor Malcolm McLaren, who was also interested in the nascent Sex Pistols. As well as a few self-composed pieces, their repertoire included approximations of 1960s beat group numbers and items by the likes of McLaren's former managerial clients, The New York Dolls.

McLaren saw at least Doll-sized potential in the Pistols, who, like other punk entertainers, were to turn out to be more like The Rolling Stones than they'd ever wanted to imagine – as acknowledged by Keith Richards: 'I loved the media thing that was happening, but, hell, we'd done that. It was a replay of 1963, 1964. I can't say I've ever listened to it because none of the cats could play. Mick Jones out of The Clash is about the only guy I can think of who I can listen to.'[4]

Almost as soon as The Clash impinged upon national consciousness, it was noticed that Jones could do nothing about a close physical resemblance to Richards – but more studied was that of New York-based punk poetess Patti Smith, so much so that she was lampooned in *New Musical Express* as a Richards clone.

Overall, Patti and others like her hadn't seemed to quite get the point. When in Chicago a few years ago, I watched a TV documentary about punk in North America. Among its talking heads was a pleasant young man with a Mohican haircut and a cultivated beard. Contrary to the UK's new-broom take on punk too, Patti Smith maintained respect for pop's elder statesmen. When, in May 1976, former Yardbird Keith Relf absorbed more than enough voltage to kill him when using a guitar fed through an unearthed amplifier, she made a reverential onstage speech that shared the inane observation that Relf had the same forename and initials as Keith Richards, still odds-on favourite as the next Big Death.

Shortly after handfuls of earth splattered onto Relf's coffin lid, a Clash B-side would include the line 'No Elvis, Beatles or Rolling Stones in 1977'. News of Presley's fatal heart attack drew a malicious cheer in a basement discotheque frequented by London punks. Benignly, many of the King's contemporaries refused to bitch back. Roy Orbison, for example, saw only 'a bunch of fresh, new people trying to do their thing like we did'.[5] Keith Richards, however, perceived that, as it had been with Brian Jones, much of the expletive-pocked obnoxiousness and casual cruelty was *épater le bourgeoisie* by middle-class youths channelling pampered frustration into pop, and coarsening themselves, perhaps prior to pulling the old Nice Lads When You Get To Know Them stroke. They felt compelled to behave in a manner that, deep down, they thought was abhorrent. 'Punks should take a few lessons in swearing,' Keith snarled, 'they don't have the stamina to be real rock stars.'[6]

In reciprocation, though, Jagger maintained that Richards was 'the original punk rocker',[7] and there was to be a – probably sardonic – exhumation of 'We Love You' by Cock Sparrer. Yet the Stones were derided by punks as bourgeois liberals with inert conservative tendencies despite the take-it-or-leave-it attitude and the margin of error that had put teeth into their music when the world was young – as epitomised by 1965's frantic 'She Said Yeah': punk or what?

There was too a certain *déjà vu* about aspects of the trendsetting Sex Pistols' career path. As many degrees beyond the Stones in outrageousness as the Stones had been beyond Presley, the Pistols became infamous for performances accompanied by violence. Like Andrew Loog Oldham had, Malcolm McLaren welcomed headline-grabbing boorishness from his charges. Following a small Top 30 beginning with a maiden single, a follow-up almost topped the UK charts. Though heard on the recording, bass player Glen Matlock had been replaced by Sid Vicious – whose dubious musicianship had been less important to the group than his assault on a gentleman of the press who had merited McLaren's displeasure.

After two more hits in 1977, the public seemed to have got over the initial shock of The Sex Pistols – even accepting them as a tolerable part of the national furniture.

During that watershed year too, amphetamines and even LSD helped fuel punk, but, as recognised in the 'get pissed, destroy!' finale of the Pistols' 'Anarchy In The UK', lager was more likely to sustain its exponents. Nevertheless, Sid Vicious was descending into a heroin hell, and an overdose was to bring about his death on 2 February 1979 while awaiting trial for the murder of Nancy Spungen, the Anita to his Keith. A morning-after comment from ex-New York Doll Johnny Thunders surfaced in *Rolling Stone*: 'Well, he beat Keith Richards for the story of the year.'[8]

Keith still made the front page with the less absolute final chapter of his own heroin odyssey. The Newport Pagnell business had come home to roost on 12 January 1977, preceded by a moment of mild comedy at a preliminary hearing in autumn with the Chairperson of Magistrates Mrs Mary Durbridge's response to the defendant's excuse for a two-hour delay owing to a laundry error, 'It appears quite extraordinary that a man of Mr Keith Richards' stature could only have one pair of trousers.'[9] At Aylesbury Crown Court, it was accepted that the LSD might have belonged to another Stone, but the cocaine hadn't, and, therefore, warranted a fine as inappreciable as the amount concerned.

This, however, was the Stamford Bridge to the Hastings that awaited Richards the following month when the idea of taping a performance before a small audience went past discussion. The 400-capacity El Mocambo club in Toronto was the chosen venue, and Keith was expected to drag himself from his Redlands pit to cross the Atlantic for rehearsals. He found this no easy task. Hours and then days passed at Toronto International Airport for those appointed to ensure his undistracted passage to the Harbour Castle Hotel and then to a downtown warehouse, which had mains leads spreading out in all directions from an encampment of guitar cases, speaker cabinets and Charlie's drum kit assembled beneath dusty strip lights.

Plane after British plane landed, and Richards would still be shuttered away in Sussex. Then, on 24 February, just over a week before the reckoning, he, Anita and Marlon shuffled through customs. When Pallenberg was instructed to open her flight bag, enough cannabis for a few spliffs and a charred spoon with a trace of heroin on it leaped out. The culprit was then hustled by peaked-capped officials out of the public gaze for an age of circular questioning and a warning that she was likely to face a heavy fine.

The incident was shrugged off as part of life's small change as the voluptuously weary couple and their son dumped their luggage in the Harbour Castle suite and trudged straight into the bedrooms for some shut-eye. The next day, a squeak of feedback from Keith's amplifier launched an unproblematic run through a mooted selection that delved as far back as their earliest Craw Daddy stumblings. Conducted by his count-ins, nods and eye contact, The Stones started to relax.

An overall mood of quiet confidence was, however, to be disrupted when, armed with a search warrant, a squad of Royal Canadian Mounted Police invaded Keith, Anita and Marlon's – supposedly bugged – hotel rooms as they lay in bed. It was so heart-sinkingly familiar: the shouting voices at the door, the uniforms, the execution of duty, the ransacking, the emptying of ashtrays into polyethylene bags, the uncovering of the dope, the monotonal caution. Keith slept through most of it, but cracked, 'I'll see you in seven years, babe.'[10] to Anita as, with a pincer-like squeeze on both arms, he was hastened outside.

Then there was the back-seat ride to the station; sitting sullen and white-faced on a wall bench; the mounting anxiety; the increasingly more aggravating whine of the air-conditioning and the illuminated desk on a raised platform where the sergeant filled in the booking slip, his eyes sweeping a now standing Keith in a subjective show of dislike. Under 'Charge', he wrote 'Possession of controlled drugs with intent to re-sell'. It was mostly heroin, and Canadian drug laws were stringent, harsh and effective, doubtlessly because of Toronto's position as a confluence of the sub-continent's trafficking thoroughfares. Richards could be facing decades in jail, reckoned the designated lawyer, although Jimi Hendrix – who'd been in precisely the same trouble in the same city eight years earlier – had convinced the jury that it had all been a terrible mistake, and had left the courthouse with a character unblemished by a felony conviction.

Like Hendrix, Richards was granted bail – chiefly on the grounds that he was either undergoing or about to undergo detoxification in a psychiatric clinic in New York. Though he'd be smiled in and out of counselling sessions, the treatment hinged principally on electro-acupuncture, which had proved successful for the similarly afflicted Pete Townshend and, in more qualified fashion, Eric Clapton.[11] 'It's a little metal box with leads that clip on to your ears,' explained Keith, 'and in two or three days – which is the worst period for kicking junk – it leaves your system. You should be incredibly sick, but you're not. Why? I don't know – because all it is is a very simple electronic nine-watt battery-run operation.'[12]

Between appointments, he convalesced in South Salem, an estate in Westchester, not quite an hour's drive outside the city limits and within close proximity to open countryside. There he'd look back at the events between arrest and bail as like a vague parody of *Midnight Express*. A drama of a US student sentenced to open-ended years in a squalid Turkish prison for a narcotics offence, it would be *the* hit movie of 1978 when, after two nail-biting postponements, Keith was scheduled to enter the dock at last on 23 October, ten days after a dazed Sid Vicious had been led from the Manhattan hotel where Nancy Spungen had died of stab wounds.

Sid's vicissitudes provoked a measure of fellow feeling in Keith, and the two generations of pop aristocracy held hands fleetingly when the Stones, understanding why the Pistols were rude about them, proffered a donation to Vicious's defence fund. To a less altruistic end, there'd also be a handful of topical ditties dedicated to the fated Sid against just one to do with Richards – 'Keith Don't Go' by Nils Lofgren – though a faction within the Stones' German fanbase marched on the Canadian Embassy in Frankfurt to present a petition asking for clemency.

This was as ineffectual as most of such strategies are, and contingency plans for life without Richards remained in force – with Jimmy Page a prime candidate to understudy him, according to media rumour. 'We all know Keith could get nothing or life imprisonment,' philosophised Mick Jagger, 'If he got life, I would carry on with the band, but I'd be very upset. I'm sure Keith could write in prison. He'd have nothing else to do.'[7]

Anticipation of the worst had already created hiccups in the negotiations for a huge deal for North American recording rights now that the Atlantic contract had run its course – though the Stones re-signed with the company for another six albums (which EMI distributed throughout the rest of the world). The first release under the new deal, *Love You Live*, was derived from tapes of the Paris Abattoirs show as well as that at the El Mocambo. At both of these, Keith had been on the rebound from a personal desolation – respectively, the death of Tara and the Toronto bust – but had found the emotional detachment to brush them aside like matchsticks, and come belligerently alive when the lights hit him.

15 The Community Servant

'I don't like to regret heroin – because I learned a lot from it. It was a large part of my life. It is something I went through and dealt with.'

– *Keith Richards*[1]

As 23 October 1978 edged closer, resolute efforts were made to present the defendant in the best possible light. Photographer Michael Putland was instructed to take 'nice, smiling pictures of Keith'[2] that tempered a pasty complexion indicative of the Dracula hours he kept: *qui male agit odit lucem.*[3] Promises were made of million-dollar endowments to drug rehabilitation charities, and press statements were circulated containing quotable gravities like, 'I have grimly determined to change my life and abstain from any drug use. I can truthfully say that the prospect of ever using drugs again is totally alien to my thinking. My experience has also had an important effect not only on my happiness, but on the happiness at home in which my son is brought up.'[1]

The whereabouts of six-year-old Dandelion was not stressed. Her removal from the public gaze had extended to her repudiating her born name and becoming 'Angela' after circumstances made it more convenient – and healthy – for her to be brought up by grandmother Doris back in Dartford where she was enrolled at the local state primary school. A subsequent passion for horse-riding was to guide her eventual entry into the world of work after a girlhood that had been relatively untraumatic, despite the tempestuous nature of her parents' lives.

Before the final act of her father's present drama unfolded in Toronto with a speed that belied the long wait, plea bargaining between defence and prosecution had resulted in a decision that he was to admit to possession on the understanding that the more heinous charge of now 'trafficking with a narcotic' wasn't to be pursued. There was, however, still more than an outside chance of a custodial sentence for all advocate Austin Cooper's argument that this 'creative, tortured person...a major contributor to art form' was a reformed character whose attempt – his fourth – to 'rid himself of this terrible problem'[4] seemed to be working. As the Stones' principal lyricist, Jagger was blamed for the detected drug references in songs such as 'Moonlight Mile', 'Can't You Hear Me Knocking', 'Torn And Frayed' and, still in the British Top 30, 'Respectable', a spin-off single from that summer's *Some Girls* album, with its line about 'taking heroin with the Duke of Kent'.

The cherry on the cake, however, was the presence in the public gallery of Rita, a blind fan with the wherewithal to have attended, purportedly, every concert of the Stones' last tour of North America. She had been noticed and befriended by Keith. This was to his unknowing benefit – for Judge Lloyd Graburn turned out to be a friend, apparently, of her family. The story of the giant of rock moved by both Rita's affliction and enthusiasm may, therefore, have had a bearing on Graburn's ruling that, as well as probation, a one-year suspended sentence and the continuation of his addiction cure, Richards was to undertake a form of community service by playing two free fundraising concerts on the same day at the Canadian Institute for the Blind's 225-seat auditorium.

Predictably, editorials in the more conservative national newspapers protested against the leniency of the sentence; some complaining about preferential treatment meted out to a celebrity when, in the same courtroom that very week, an otherwise nondescript teenager caught with a smaller amount of a softer drug had received three months gaol. The volume of outrage was sufficiently loud for the Canadian Crown Prosecution to be granted an eventual hearing at the Ontario Court of Appeal, and it was to take until the following September for Keith to be completely off the hook on the submission that prison was likely to precipitate a relapse.

It had helped, too, that Richards had already fulfilled his most unusual legal obligation on 21 April 1979. Advisedly, the venue had been switched to the more capacious Oshawa Civic Stadium to limit the danger of both riot and the scalping by touts of a crowd heaving with both those with the blessing of sight and a minority who could hear the sounds, but would not see The Rolling Stones give their only performances that year – following a build-up by master-of-ceremonies John Belushi, comedy actor and star of *The Blues Brothers*, a movie then in post-production. [5]

Belushi also introduced the newly formed support act. The New Barbarians was the brainchild of Ron Wood and Keith. Its purpose was to showcase the former's latest solo album, *Gimme Some Neck* – and, perhaps, to provide the latter with occupational therapy by banishing convalescent sloth, and catapulting him back onto the concert bulletin while the Stones were off the road. Described by Richards as a 'moonshine group', The New Barbarians' core personnel was completed by the ubiquitous Bobby Keyes, New Orleans drummer Ziggy Modeliste from The Meters (who bore comparison to Booker T And The MGs in style, as US chart contenders and as an all-purpose backing combo), Ian McLagan, The Faces' keyboard player [6] and, on bass, jazz-rock wizard Stanley Clarke.

During the immediate sell-out US tour that followed the Oshawa bash – and when illustrated on the *Buried Alive* bootleg and the official *Live* album – though the set conjured up flashes of ersatz Stones sorcery, these were approximations within the loose, almost sketchy luxury of a certain self-indulgence. While

Keith sang 'Happy' and 'Before They Make Me Run' – his party-piece on *Some Girls*, and very much based on recent events – and he and Ron duetted on 'Love In Vain', the chief repertory source was *Gimme Some Neck*. A few blown riffs, flurries of bum notes, vaguely apocalyptic cadences, yelled directives and a lot of amorphous jamming were reported as well as much in-joking and off-mic swapping of banter, but the general feeling, as cigarettes were lit and beer-can rings pulled in the dressing room afterwards, was that, if the proceedings had been as much for the benefit of the musicians as the customers, it had been fun for both. Furthermore, it had to be admitted that the overall presentation was becoming punchier as the final date – at the Forum in Los Angeles on 21 May – approached.

In the cold light of the next day, some ticket holders wondered why they'd bothered. Whatever the opinions about the music, sometimes the outfit wasn't even the full shilling in other respects. British session player Phil Chen deputising for Clarke was tolerated, and guest appearances by Sarah Dash from LaBelle and Sugar Blue, mouth-organist on disco-smitten 'Miss You' – the first *Some Girls* 45 – was welcomed, but at a return booking at Milwaukee's Sports Arena in the New Year, there was piqued uproar with the realisation that Richards – and McLagan – were nowhere to be seen.

While the ensemble had been quorate at the Knebworth Festival the previous August – their sole British date – it had garnered faint praise at most in post-punk music press. As expressive as the most vitriolic of these was Mick Jones's pithy, if predetermined, dismissal of his lookalike's dreary return to the British stage with not just a 'dinosaur band', but one that was almost a 'supergroup', that most fascist of pop cliques.

Nevertheless, barrages of whistling, cheering and stamping had greeted The New Barbarians before they'd played a note back in the USA, where consumers were less discriminating about a dinosaur band with moonlighting Rolling Stones in it. There, punk had appealed mainly to curiosity seekers until the grubbing music industry had stolen its most viable ideas and got its more palatable executants to ease up, talk correct and get ready to rake in the loot. Once of London's sub-Pistols Generation X, the appositely named Billy Idol, for instance, was no Scott Walker as a vocalist, but he was to score in the US dream-date stakes, having been groomed as an updated Ricky Nelson.

Yet bedrock US punk, if doomed to be rudderless, battled on in desperate anachronisms like Darby Crash and his Germs from a well-to-do Los Angeles suburb.[7] After engagements in city clubs, they'd graduated to opening for the likes of Blondie and Devo, and a projected evolution into a sort of parochial 'answer' to The Sex Pistols. Being enormous along Sunset Strip was enormous enough for the Germs – but the overreaching Darby's exploratory visit to London put the tin-lid on the group. Looking a right plonker with an Adam Ant white stripe across his nose, a homecoming Crash fronted a poorly received new outfit a few weeks before a one-shot Germs reunion and then his self-administered death via a surfeit of heroin – just like Sid Vicious.

There but for fortune – and the intervention of Canadian law – had gone Keith Richards, debatably, the daddy of all stimulant-related pop casualties, but still transcending the slings and arrows of every chemical that impinged upon his psyche. While he'd finished with heroin, a cocaine and vodka binge had brightened idle hours on The New Barbarians' dates – as had dalliances with his travelling companion, Lily Wenglass, a Scandinavian model.

This new love was known to Anita, who'd feigned aloofness to retain composure in the aftershock of the Toronto bother when, 'Our lawyer lectured us that we were a bad influence on each other, and that if we were ever going to kick heroin, we would have to separate. That really ended it for us, although we occasionally saw each other for the sake of the children.'[8]

Secluded in South Salem, she made light of whatever leaked to her about her common-law husband's infidelity. After all, she'd hardly lived like a nun since he'd been away. It hadn't taken long for every room to look as if a hand grenade had been tossed into it. Not only was the place a tip, but an interrelated fug wafted out whenever the front door was answered. As for Anita herself, she'd put on weight alarmingly, most obviously in a visage of waxen pallor and bloated by the excesses of her youth.

Yet the aura of the Fascinating Older Woman had captivated a 17-year-old neighbour, Scott Cantrell. By the evening of 20 July 1979, the attraction was mutual enough for him to be lying on her bed while watching a televised commemoration of Neil Armstrong's small step. Nonetheless, the *New York Post* was to cobble together a contrived article about a coven to which Pallenberg and Cantrell were linked – like, Salem was the scene of that famous witch-hunt in 1692, wasn't it? There were also unfounded allegations of the sacrifice of missing family pets, what were not normal late-night screams and Anita keeping a vampire bat and corrupting local youngsters with cocaine and sexual favours. These and further stretchers had been fabricated after police had hastened Scott to Northern Westchester Hospital with a gunshot wound in his head. Minutes after midnight on 21 July, the unhappy youth's feeble breathing slackened and he was gone.

During consequent hours of questioning, Keith rang from France and Anita repeated to detectives her insistence that, while she was occupied with housework, Scott's worrying pastime of playing Russian roulette had backfired. It transpired too that his mother had committed suicide on the previous Christmas Day. As twilight thickened, a prototypical headline chalked on evening newspaper kiosks was 'PROBE ASKED IN BEDROOM DEATH AT STONE HOME'. Chief among those doing the asking were Cantrell's father and elder brother, 'What was this woman doing, tidying the bedroom at 10.30 at night? There is something very fishy about this. A thirty-seven-year-old woman should have known better than to associate with a seventeen-

KEITH RICHARDS

year-old boy. Police are saying that it was a self-inflicted wound, but I don't believe Scott would do such a thing. I think they were lovers, and that she had supplied him with drugs.'⁹

Circumstances were suspicious enough for Pallenberg's passport to be confiscated, but a Westchester court was to clear her of any involvement in young Cantrell's death – though his family continued to think otherwise. However, a misdemeanour charge of possessing the unlicenced revolver that did the damage was upheld, and a fine imposed.

Keith was angry at the loss of the gun – a Smith-and-Wesson he'd bought in Florida – but had chosen otherwise to remove himself, geographically at least, from the action in Westchester. After the New Barbarians US tour had wound down, a footloose period of excursions back and forth across the Atlantic was notable for sightings of Richards perhaps at the Bottom Line in Greenwich Village, sharing a backstage joke with McGuinn-Clark-Hillman, a reconstitution of three-fifths of the original Byrds. There he was again with Ron Wood, ambling across the boards at the Elysee Matignon in Paris to shake hands with Leonard Bernstein during an extravaganza in honour of the composer of *West Side Story*, who'd planted successful feet in both the classical and pop camps.

Flattered that they should ask, Richards was also assisting on albums by such respected names as Steve Cropper – Booker T's guitarist – and Peter Tosh, now an artiste in his own right too. Keith had already dabbled in a solo project himself – a single coupling self-produced tracks taped whenever studio time had gone begging over the past two years.

With Ian Stewart and Mick Taylor's drummer, Mike Driscoll, the A-side was a fiery revival of a 1960 Chuck Berry B-side, 'Run Rudolph Run'. Since Bing Crosby's 'White Christmas' had sold by the ton in 1942, the Christmas single has been, with the 'death disc', one of pop's hardiest forms. Gene Autry, The Goons, Dickie Valentine, Elvis Presley, The Beverley Sisters,

Freddie And The Dreamers, Max Bygraves, Slade, John Lennon, Wizzard, Jethro Tull and Showaddywaddy had been among multitudinous entertainers trying their luck with seasonal platters aimed directly at a time of year when the usual chart rules don't apply. How else had Valentine's 'Christmas Alphabet' knocked 'Rock Around The Clock' from Number One in Britain in December 1955? Why did repromotions of Slade's 'Merry Christmas Everybody' keep registering in the list years after the disc's optimum moment in 1973?

'Run Rudolph Run' had all the credentials of a Yuletide smash, but none that actually grabbed the public – mainly because it missed the December sell-in altogether, issued as it was in February 1979. Though it tumbled into the bargain bin, Keith seemed to have enjoyed committing this old favourite to vinyl. Others better known for their own compositions were also releasing non-originals in the mid- to late 1970s, either to display their skills as 'interpreters' or simply because they were running out of ideas. Bryan Ferry, Jonathan King, John Lennon and The Hollies had all issued entire LPs of oldies after David Bowie had set the ball rolling with 1973's *Pin-Ups*, an affectionate trawl through British beat group classics. Renewed interest in 1960s instrumentals had put veteran guitarist Bert Weedon abruptly at the top of the British album list in 1976 with *22 Golden Guitar Greats*. There were also singles of old chestnuts by the likes of Zoot Money, Traffic's Jim Capaldi, The Troggs (an incredible 'Good Vibrations') and Colin Blunstone of The Zombies.

Keith compounded his own retrospection with a cover of Jimmy Cliff's 'The Harder They Come', demonstrating an adept absorption of that chopping reggae afterbeat, on the flip-side of 'Run Rudolph Run'. It had been realised during sessions for *Emotional Rescue*, the album that followed *Some Girls*, in Hollywood. However, a ten-minute reggae-flavoured Jagger-Richards item, the hitherto-unissued 'Jah Is Not Dead', was finished at Chris Blackwell's lavish new Compass Point Studios in the Bahamas in 1979 when Keith was working with both Peter Tosh and Black Uhuru, an ensemble created by some of Tosh's sidemen – including drummer Sly Dunbar (the 'Sly' in Sly And The Revolutionaries) and Robbie Shakespeare, whose lithely contrapuntal bass was as much a vehicle of melody as rhythm. If James Brown, a bandleader of some discernment, reckoned that they had no idea, Sly and Robbie were an automatic choice for Bob Dylan, Serge Gainsbourg and other non-Caribbean pop stars wanting to try reggae.

Some block-booked Blue Wave, the Barbados complex that had been purchased by multi-instrumentalist Eddie Grant from his chart entries in the late 1960s with London's multi-racial Equals, and maintained with his earnings as a solo hit-maker in the 1970s. It was among considerations as somewhere to rehearse when Richards and Jagger holidayed on the island early in 1981 while pondering The Rolling Stones' comeback as the world's top touring band after an interregnum of more than two cliff-hanging years.

16 The Birthday Boy

'Rock 'n' roll has lasted because nothing else has come along.'

– Keith Richards[1]

In the war against adverse acoustics, weapons such as programmable desks and graphic equalisers couldn't erase the perturbing psychological undertow compounded by the bald fact of John Lennon's slaying on a New York pavement by a so-called admirer in December 1980. Mark David Chapman had also been noticed sniffing round Bob Dylan. Like mafia dons, pop stars of the same magnitude were edgy when approached by even the most mild-mannered strangers. 'John's shooting definitely scared all of us,' admitted George Harrison. 'When a fan recognises me and rushes over, it definitely makes me nervous.'[2]

Once seen but rarely outside either his apartment facing Central Park or his various rural and coastal retreats, a fit-looking 40-year-old John had no longer been ploughing energy into keeping out of the limelight that autumn, and was talking about a return to the stage. Among those who'd been beseeching him to emerge from Rip Van Winkle-esque vocational slumber had been Keith Richards. 'When we were rehearsing in New York, we tried to find John Lennon, and get him back into the scene. I mean, what is John Lennon doing, farming cows in upstate New York?'[3]

Now, by embarking on a tenth US tour in autumn 1981, the Stones were going to be even more vulnerable than the ex-Beatle to stalking by autograph hunters with guns. Yet, while security was stepped up, Jagger spoke for the group: 'You can't spend your life being paranoid. There'll always be nutters, and you just have you watch out for them.'[1] Death would still lurk in the skies too as the Stones crossed the sub-continent in a Boeing 707, but the only fatalities were beyond the crash barriers – a teenage girl falling 50 feet from the gallery in Seattle's Kingdome and a young man whose life puddled out of him during an altercation with a spiv with forged tickets outside the auditorium in Houston.

Yet, to those for whom reality was based on columns of figures, the expedition with its vast and peripatetic 'official' merchandising outlet was a howling success from start to finish. Less than a fortnight before opening night at Philadelphia's JFK Stadium on 25 September, if a dim view had been taken of a local radio station's exposure of a hush-hush water-testing concert in Sir Morgan's Cave, a small club in Worcester, Massachusetts, the upset was turned to advantage via the ensuing publicity when police riot control – involving helicopters – tried to contain the convergence on the place of a crowd that could have filled it ten times over. Gleeful ramming and savage oaths as the mob tried to break in were assuaged when the doors were flung open and the Stones were heard, if not seen, by everyone.

Keith's would be the most quoted remark afterwards: 'It was probably better than we thought. Technically, it was really rough. It was as if we were playing the Station Hotel in 1963. You don't forget those things. It was sort of like, "Well, we did it then. We can do it now."'[1] This was believable and alluring enough for the stop at San Francisco's Candlestick Park to draw the biggest open-air audience in the city's history. An extra date had been added – in Rockford, Illinois – as the result of a petition of nearly 40,000 signatures to tour promoter Bill Graham. Furthermore, Keith's 38th birthday (with Marlon,

Angela and Doris flown in for the celebration) coincided with the televised transmission of a show in Virginia to most major North American cities.

Pictured on the front cover of a mid-tour edition of *Rolling Stone*, and voted best instrumentalist in that periodical's readers' poll for the year, Keith seemed astounded by 'everyone making such a fuss about a bunch of middle-aged madmen going on tour'.[1] All the same, it was he who'd been most vocal in advocating the inclusion of support acts from the very dawn of modern pop. After he'd pitched in with Etta James on a rendition of 'Miss You' during her season at New York's Lone Star Cafe, the singer of 1955's 'Dance With Me Henry' – an 'answer' to Hank Ballard And The Midnighters' risqué 'Work With Me Annie' – opened the show at Cleveland; but more prestigious was Screamin' Jay Hawkins doing likewise for two nights at Madison Square Garden where all 200,000 seats had sold out in mere hours.

Two years earlier, Richards had assisted on Jay's torrid remake of 'I Put A Spell On You', which had more to do with James Brown sex machine than the blood-chilling dementia of the 1956 original. More typical of Hawkins during this period, however, were standards like 'Ebb Tide', 'I've Got You Under My Skin' and 'Time After Time', arranged in mid-1970s 'Philly Soul' fashion with synthesised strings, chukka-wukka guitars and prominent female chorale. These are layered by Jay's non-screamin' baritone, which betrayed more individuality on more in-yer-face numbers such as 'Africa Gone Funky'.

Overall, Hawkins acquitted himself well, made nice music. Yet the image of the manic, witch doctoresque figure of old was too impossible to forget, thus reducing 'Ebb Tide', 'Africa Gone Funky' and so forth to a *faux pas* of an attempt to adapt enough of prevailing trends to not turn off older fans. Better suited for the intimacy of theatre or club than stadiums designed for championship sport, his subtleties were wasted anyway on a mob impatient for the main attraction. Most professionally, nevertheless, he flogged his time-honoured turn for all it was worth until the usual smoke-filled exit and weak applause from onlookers hardened by years of excesses by Bobby 'Boris' Pickett, The Crazy World Of Arthur Brown, Dr John, Black Sabbath, Alice Cooper, The Cramps and others for whom Screamin' Jay's pioneering accomplishments had been received wisdom.

Despite his endeavours on Hawkins' behalf going awry, Keith Richards lent his celebrity to further the causes of other of his childhood heroes, both alive and dead. He was a laconic 'talking head' on *The Real Buddy Holly Story*, a documentary screened on BBC 2 in 1985, but this was a mere bagatelle compared to what should have been his finest hour in this respect: *Hail! Hail! Rock 'N' Roll*, the sanctification of Chuck Berry's 60th birthday on celluloid and in the back-slapping attendance by himself and other celebrities who'd grown up to the Brown-Eyed if now less Handsome Man's music.

Symptomatic too of further public patronages of pop's methuselahs in the mid-1980s were similarly glittering spectaculars in honour of Fats Domino and 53-year-old Carl Perkins in the midst of devout guests that included Ron Wood, Eric Clapton and a couple of ex-Beatles. Roy Orbison's turn would come in 1987 at Los Angeles' Coconut Ballroom with the likes of Ry Cooder, Tom Waits and Elvis Costello helping out.

The idea of *Hail! Hail! Rock 'N' Roll* had come to Keith on 23 January the previous year when he inducted Berry at the first ever Rock And Roll Hall Of Fame ceremony. Mounting the podium at New York's deluxe Wardorf-Astoria Hotel, Keith, with several stiff drinks on board, delivered a heartfelt citation ('I lifted every lick he ever played') and presented the statuette. Later, the stage heaved with stars and starlets for an 'impromptu' valedictory jam. Amid the musical clutter that characterised such affairs, Keith caught several bars of unadulterated magic when

Chuck was able to take over at the central microphone. Eyes met and telepathic communication seemed to read, 'I know you and you know me. We understand each other in a secret way.' The idol and his worshipper had become as one.

Chuck had not assumed such an instant if covert intimacy with Keith during earlier encounters. In 1971, Keith – albeit encouraged by backstage staff – had had the sauce to plug in his guitar and trespass onstage during a Berry recital in Hollywood. There are conflicting accounts of what happened next. Chuck would recall that 'I thought the cat had something, but I couldn't recognise him. After a song, I said to play softer, play down. So I start the song, and it's loud. On the next song, I just said, "Off!". Then my secretary is off-stage, screaming at me, "That's Keith Richards!".'[1] Mick Jagger, however, was to confide to a journalist's cassette recorder that, 'Keith wanted to get up and jam with Chuck, who said, "Forget it", but Keith got up anyway, just walked on in the middle of a song. When Chuck saw him, he walked over and bopped him in the eye, gave him a huge shiner.'[4]

Jagger may have been confused about the location of this lamentable incident because another tale was that, ten years later, at the Ritz in New York, Richards trooped backstage and attempted to natter with proud familiarity to Berry, who swivelled round and, after staring at him, almost with dislike for a split-second – as if he resented the adoration – let fly a punch that met Keith's face. Though reminded by his entourage of which Stone he had assaulted, Berry apologised, apparently, to Ron Wood. Well, they all look the same, these long-haired Limeys.

The bruise had healed and so had the pride that Berry had twisted into a frown by the time the Rock And Roll Hall Of Fame junket was over. Somehow, Keith wanted to recapture and protract the sensation of those few moments at the big finish because 'I felt I owed him so much.'[5] Contacting an unexpectedly genial Chuck before the week was out, he enthused about the feasibility of either a bio-pic or a project along the lines of *The Real Buddy Holly Story*.

Consequent brainstorming boiled down to the pencilling in of a Berry concert in his hometown of St Louis to tie in with the publication of his autobiography. The results were to be immortalised on film – with Keith overseeing a thoroughly drilled all-star backing combo rather than trusting his hero's usual policy of employing a pick-up group that, with little or no time to rehearse or even sound check with their paymaster, would be chastised for musical errors rather than the jet-legged legend fronting them. He was the genuine article, wasn't he? What did the too-youthful provincial oiks behind him know about classic rock?

Worth quoting at length are the abridged recollections – in Runyon-esque present tense – of a Berry soirée in Paris by one such hireling, British bass guitarist Garry Jones:

A month before the gig, I've invested in a cassette of Mr Berry's Greatest Hits, *and have proceed to transcribe and learn them. A week previously, there's a showing on television of some dreadful Mr Berry gig. We all religiously watch it, looking for hints. Pat Thomas, the pianist, laughs and explains that all the songs are in four keys – E♭, B♭, G or C. This doesn't correlate with the cassette.*

All afternoon in Paris, the promoter's functionaries are informing us of Mr Berry's progress – on the 'plane, in France, in a taxi, in a hotel, on his way to the gig – a large marquee in a grassy, railed rectangle, somewhere to the north of the city. Backstage left is for the band, backstage right is for Mr Berry. Progress reports continue, and the band sound-check without Mr Berry.

The band are summoned into Mr Berry's dressing room about half an hour before showtime. We're introduced. Mr Berry explains that all his songs are, indeed, in the keys of E♭,

B♭ , G or C – so my heart sinks. Wearing a shirt that defines the word 'garishness', Mr Berry picks up a 1950s ES345 guitar to demonstrate, and it's horrendously out of tune.

Me: 'Do you want to borrow my tuner?'

Mr Berry: 'Are you calling me ugly, boy?'

Me: stammering noises.

Mr Berry is pleased that he's got a 'brother' in the band (Pat's black). Mr Berry explains how we have to watch his left foot as the indicator of what's going on.

Simon Price (drummer): 'What's the first song going to be?'

Mr Berry: 'I don't know, but the last'll be "Reelin' And Rockin'".'

With all that help, we are dismissed to wait for the lights to go down.

There's some introduction. I'm stage left, staring at Mr Berry's left hand and left foot. Mr Berry starts a Mr Berry riff, and I'm trying to calculate what key he's playing that riff in. From the position of his left hand, it looks like G, so I've got a one in four chance of not looking a complete twat. Mr Berry gurns for the punters he seems to despise, and revolves round the band to tell them to simplify what they're playing: everything will end up like a Status Quo tribute band doing Mr Berry covers. He plays piano with Pat to explain dumbing-down (Pat's the greatest piano player in the known physical universe). Left foot, left hand. Left foot, left hand. Slow blues because he's having such a good time: 'It Hurts

Me Too' by Elmore James. Left foot, left hand. Left foot, left hand. Mr Berry's friend has been stage right all the time with a watch. After fifty-odd minutes, 'Reelin' And Rockin'' is signalled, and it's ES345 behind the head, duck-walking slowly offstage. On the signalled hour, he's off.

With more time and greater means than Garry, Keith was determined to do whatever willingness and energy would do to give the best of everything to his first authorised stint on the boards with Berry. More than a week of rehearsals at the fellow's house in Wentzville on the outskirts of St Louis were, however, freighted with Richards' ruthlessness at sticking to the task in hand and Berry's alternate grouchiness and bored indolence as if he couldn't wait to knock off for the day from some run-of-the-mill job he'd done for decades – which it was. As musical director, Keith bit back on an understandable exasperation when affronted by the criticisms and reprimands that preceded withdrawals into abstracted indifference. His hackles rose time and time again, but he was determined not to stride out, insulted, to pour himself a whiskey and dissect the host's character and ability with bitter intensity.

On the night, only naked pleas would cajole Chuck to test vocal balance for Johnnie Johnson, Bobby Keyes and the rest of the hand-picked instrumentalists from every trackway of his career, and the special guests, among them Eric Clapton, Julian Lennon and Etta James, who'd agreed to appear at the Fox. This was the theatre where Berry's teenage self had been refused admission in an age when any admixture of Negro blood was deemed sufficient to restrict its owner to 'colored' public conveniences and launderettes not displaying the sign 'Whites Only Or Maids In Uniform'.

This time, Chuck Berry stepped beneath its very proscenium, and an almost palpable wave of goodwill washed over him as it always did, regardless of who shared the same stage. With a dotage rich in material comforts earned from a golden past, Berry had nothing to lose by serving his present accompanists as he had Garry Jones *et al*, launching impetuously into songs not in the ordered *modus operandi*, changing keys mid-song if he felt like it, and ripping prescribed arrangements to pieces, leaving a panicking Keith and the others to busk behind him. Like, what key's this one in, man? Like Z minus, man.

Yet, from theoretical disaster came forth a hysterical gaiety, with cavorting onlookers assuming the role of rhythm section during the up-tempo rockers, and Chuck tumbling about, skylarking and pulling out every ham trick in the book, guarding his pride of place with the passionate venom of a six-year-old with a new bike. Well before he reached 'Reelin' And Rockin'', he'd been home and dry.

All's well that ended well, Keith supposed and, before the fond gaze of those in the green room, he and Chuck had bear-hugged each other, but 'I couldn't warm to him if I was cremated next to him – a big chip on his shoulder and, now and again, it's knocked off, and he's a fascinating, sweet guy, but suddenly he checks himself like he's given away too much, having too much fun, and the armour goes back on.'[6]

The experience faded, and Richards was so able to disassociate music with the individual personal weaknesses of its practitioners that he remained as well meaning when trying to throw down a line to other olde-tyme rock 'n' rollers. Recovery from a near-fatal stomach operation had caused a lengthy halt to Jerry Lee Lewis's concert schedule as well as his refusal of a kind invitation to play on the Stones' *Undercover* album in 1983. Yet Richards – along with Dave Davies, Van Morrison, Fleetwood Mac's Mick Fleetwood and other illustrious fans paid pragmatic respects to the Killer by joining him on the boards at various junctures – 'maybe the last chance', reckoned Keith[7] – throughout a decade blighted by the alleged marital ructions that led to Lewis's sudden withdrawal from a UK visit. For all the maturity inherent in ol' Jerry Lee's latter-day recordings, little seemed to have changed since his breakthrough in the rockin' 1950s.

Keith's own domestic upheavals were the subject of media speculation too. He and Anita had made their separation official, but their continued amity was exemplified by his presence at Marlon's 14th birthday party at her new home on Long Island.

As Anita faded into the background of his life, a shadowy figure from his adolescence reared up in sharper focus. In contrast to John Lennon's errant father, Bert Richards had been too self-esteeming to sell his story to a Sunday newspaper or have his hands open for any further bounties that might trickle, indirectly or otherwise, from his affinity to a wealthy pop group. Bert had had nothing to show for this when, in spring 1982, *The News Of The World* reported that he and his only child had spoken for the first time since before 'Come On' in 1963. While Keith hadn't risked discomforting Doris by being chummy with her long-lost former spouse, over the years there had been 'a card here, a letter there. I'd send a note, and a year later, I'd get a reply – because he never knew where to send anything because I'd be in one country one minute, another the next – or I'd be under arrest.

'I was thinking all the time that he doesn't want to know me. I've grown up to be the exact opposite of what he wanted me to be. Eventually, we got back together in ''82 around the end of that tour. We'd been communicating a bit more over the month before, and I said, "Come down to my place." So he agreed, and I was waiting for the guy I left behind twenty years ago. I expected him to get out of the car and – boom! – smash me in the teeth. That's how screwed up I was about it. At the time, it was a deep emotional thing, nothing you could really detect on the surface. Then the car door opened, and out stepped this little old guy. I thought, "That's my Dad." He came up and said, "Hello, son, How're you doing?" – and I'm breaking up already.

Then I knew that it would be all right. He lives up the road now, and we have a game of dominoes some Fridays. I go up there, and we have bangers-and-mash.'[5]

The reunion had been encouraged by a woman with whom Richards had been noticed in public with increasing frequency since their introduction by Jerry Hall, the soon-to-be second Mrs Jagger, at New York's Roxy Roller Disco on the occasion of Keith's 36th birthday. She was Patti Hansen, whose tall, firm-breasted profile and avalanche of wavy blonde tresses had been the key to a career in catwalks and cloth since leaving her Staten Island school in 1973. Now in the same professional league as her matchmaking friend Jerry – a model in international demand – Patti was also making headway as a film actor. At a loose end, Keith was hovering off-camera when she was in San Francisco for a part in *Hard To Hold*. *Citizen Kane* it wasn't, but the general verdict was that Patti had coped well with a fair-to-middling flick.

However strange a choice this English rock 'n' roller may have seemed on first acquaintance, Patti's elderly, church-going parents had raised no objections when she announced that she wanted to marry the boy. His name now linked with hers in high-society gossip columns too, Keith seemed as fondly in love as he could be of a beautiful and talented girlfriend 14 years his junior. Nobody was getting any younger, but the misery of the final years with Anita had deferred to a breezy vitality, amazing to those who hadn't seen much of him since the dopey 1970s.

Reader, Keith Richards and Patti Hansen tied the knot quietly on 8 December 1983 at the Finnesterra Hotel at Cabo San Lucas, Mexico, on Keith's 40th birthday. The best man – and the only other Stone there – was Mick, who may have remembered his own nuptials before TV crews and the world's press during the sojourn in France.

The relative secrecy of Keith and Patti's union was a gesture of defiance against a nosy world – which would know nothing either of two daughters until after they had been born.

Theodora Dupree on 18 March 1985, with Keith attending a labour for the first time, and Alexandra Nicole, also in New York, on 28 July 1986, delivered by a doctor who, while the father held the baby, just minutes old, in his arms, asked for a signature on five Stones albums.

The doctor had wondered why the group hadn't appeared on *Live Aid*, a major landmark on rock's road to respectability, the previous summer. They had, nevertheless, been represented in the satellite-linked outside broadcast from JFK Stadium when Mick duetted with Tina Turner, and Keith and Ron picked their six-strings to Bob Dylan's allocated three numbers, 'The Ballad Of Hollis Brown', 'When The Ship Comes In' (with its 'the whole wide world is watching' line) and the one-size-fits-all pacifist opus 'Blowin' In The Wind', all dredged up from his Greenwich Village beginnings when the civil rights movement had fused with folk song to be labelled 'protest'.

Theoretically, this selection of songs was most apposite – especially 'Blowin' In The Wind'. I mean, like, *war is wrong*. People get *killed*, you know. Within the unseen millions of viewers at home and the crowd actually in the grounds at Philadelphia, many may have wept in anticipation of Dylan, pop's single most enigmatic and messianic symbol of hipness, brushing aside like chaff all that had gone before – Queen, David Bowie, a reformed Who and Led Zeppelin, The Beach Boys, Mick and Tina, you name 'em. Yet the minstrel-to-a-generation and his accomplices snatched a shambling near-catastrophe from the jaws of certain triumph. It wasn't easy: they started with the optimum moment in the show; an audience that wanted to like them; a sincere introductory eulogy from Oscar-winning Jack Nicholson, bereft of his customary jocularities; a welcoming bedlam of applause for simply existing and repeated opportunities to save the situation.

To be fair, it might have defied a resurrected John Lennon not to have been a disappointment. Yet the anti-climax that was

Dylan, Richards and Wood was only almost-but-not-quite the pig's ear it became when the myth gripped harder, and even the rottenest reviews didn't diminish them to the diehard fan, who lapped up as the prerogative of glamour their mistakes and deficiencies – plectrums dropped from fumbling fingers, the snapped guitar strings, pinpricks of sweat on the timid songbird's forehead, cigarettes drooping lazily from Keith's and Ron's lips and the apologetic grins as they delivered notes they thought they'd fluffed but, played back, were safely adequate.

Afterwards, too, Keith emptied his lungs with a *whoosh* and stated the case for the defence. 'The reason I did it was because Bob turned up at Ronnie Wood's place, and we had some amazing rehearsals. The fact is that to go on at the time we did, just before the end, with three acoustic guitars is madness – and not having worked together on stage before, we didn't know what to expect. I still really enjoyed it, you know. It was completely off the cuff. Strings were breaking, and Bob's a nervous guy, and he's looking around, worrying – and there were guys just off stage, tuning up electric guitars for the finale. That's all we could hear, so we were playing absolutely deaf.'[5]

He also slipped in the distressing news that 'the Stones were asked to play it, but they weren't a band anymore anyway. They'd already broken up.'[5]

17 The Distant Friend

'One of the reasons this band has stayed together for so long is that they don't socialise. It's like if you worked at a bank. You wouldn't necessarily hang out with the other tellers, would you?'

– Arnold Dunn (road manager)[1]

It was at that point in life where time is marked by the first deaths of those of your own over-the-hill generation. Extramural activities aside, the most absolute rationale for the gang to break up had been Ian Stewart's fatal coronary in December 1985. 'I thought he'd be the one to hold the shovel, the one to bury us all,' brooded Keith. 'What a hole he's left – such an obvious gap.'[2]

There were still the Glimmer Twins, remaining behind to minister to mixing and other production chores after the others had gone home, but Keith and Mick were no longer as inseparable as they once were. The former's perspective was that 'up until the beginning of the 1980s, you could have called me up at the North Pole and Mick at the South Pole, and we would have said the same thing. We were that close. I didn't change, but he did. He became obsessed with age – his own and others. I don't see the point of pretending that you are twenty-five when you're not.'[3]

Increasingly longer periods between tours had loosened professional bonds too. On the run around the world, the two old pals couldn't help but get together to work up songs for the Stones from only a title or fragment of melody, but, often dwelling in different continents now, they tended to present each other with songs in more advanced states of completion than before. By the mid-1980s, it had become 'Jagger and Richards' rather than 'Jagger-Richards' with either functioning as the other's session man, staying away when not needed – just as it had been for Lennon, McCartney, Harrison and Starr when night had fallen on The Beatles.

Tellingly, the first Stones A-side from an external source since 1964's 'Little Red Rooster' was issued in 1986. A fixture on Keith's car cassette player, Bob and Earl's 'Harlem Shuffle' was, he said, 'probably the first disco record. It was still the early 1960s when they did it, but the sound and beat were very connectable to that early disco stuff.'[4] While he'd first heard it throbbing in the Scotch Of St James, the Bag O' Nails and like London in-clubs in the dear, dead Swinging Sixties, 'Harlem Shuffle' had been a 'sleeper' hit in 1969 after it had found its way time and time again onto the turntable at Up The Junction in Crewe, Stoke-on-Trent's Golden Torch and other early storm centres of what was to coalesce as 'northern soul' when Wigan's celebrated Casino Soul Club opened in 1973. This venue attracted a membership of around 100,000, including regular weekend dancers from as far away as Southampton who sported 'suedehead' crops and the Casino male's obligatory uniform of bowling shirt, brogue footwear and ridiculously baggy trousers.

However, the northern soul scene and disco fever in general had become sufficiently passé for the Stones' revival of 'Harlem Shuffle' to bring much of the aura of a fresh sensation to the charts, climbing to Number 13 in Britain and 5 in the USA. It was followed by 'One Hit (To The Body)', a Jagger-Richards-Wood creation that floundered in both Top 40s' lower reaches. Each single had been lifted from *Dirty Work*, an album that, by Keith's estimation, had been 'deliberately structured so that every number could be played live, simply, easy'.[5] He'd been metaphorically rubbing his hands with the contemplation of recording sessions, having predicted to anyone listening a second golden age of back-to-back 'Satisfaction'-'Get Off Of My Cloud'-proportioned smash hits for the Stones. 'Then we finished the record,' he sighed, 'and Mick suddenly said, "I ain't going on no road" – so that was the rug pulled from under me.'[5]

Though 'Lonely At The Top', co-written with Richards in 1979, was to open *She's The Boss*, Jagger's first solo album, Keith's discontent about this enterprise taking precedent over the new Stones album and interrelated tour had permitted, apparently, more than a little offhand breast beating to intrude upon a couple of remaindered *Dirty Work* pieces sung by Richards himself. These were 'Treat Me Like A Fool' and 'Knock Your Teeth Out One By One', perhaps an extrapolated variant of a naked threat: 'If Mick tours without the band, I'll slit his throat.'[3]

Jagger countered with, 'Occasionally, you want to strangle even the closest of friends',[5] and the two staged a fight for the benefit of hovering media during the shoot of the 'One Hit' video. This was passed off as a bit of a lark, but storm clouds were gathering. The possibility that Jagger might slip his cable permanently may have been as real as it was for all four Beatles, who, however reluctantly or unknowingly, had been well into solo careers long before their partnership had been dissolved in the High Court.

Food for thought too was the far more recent disbandment of another 1960s outfit, seemingly built to last, through the defection of one of its interlocking personalities. The Searchers' decade in chicken-in-a-basket-type cabaret had been interrupted by two well-received albums of new material in the late 1970s, and their presentation remained a vibrant recreation of the overall mood of the 1960s beat boom with a return to the charts never out of the question. In 1985, however, singing guitarist Mike Pender left the group to front 'Mike Pender's Searchers'. His departure was considered regrettable but by no means disastrous by the 'official' Searchers, who continued with a replacement. However, the situation was complicated further four years later by the first manifestation of a combo fronted by Tony Jackson, lead vocalist on The Searchers' first hits – and biggest US smash, 'Love Potion Number Nine'.[6]

While it was unlikely that customers would also be obliged to pay their money and take a choice between The Rolling Stones and Mick Jagger's Rolling Stones – with maybe Mick Taylor leading an ensemble earning ovations with versions of Stones classics on which he may or may not have been heard – Keith was long-faced about Mick's now open preparations for solo dates in Japan and Australasia, 'I couldn't deal with it any more. It's like a marriage. Friction builds up over the years.'[6]

Keith was driven beyond desultory sabre-rattling. With drummer Paul Shaffer – from NBC's satirical *Saturday Night Live*'s resident musicians – and session bass player Marcus Miller, he registered a protest of sorts by delivering old Stones numbers with rueful affection on the same television channel's *Friday Night Videos*.

Sibling rivalry was to intensify to railing at each other in the press, sometimes with almost audible sniggers, and even in record grooves. To what extent it was sincere, grist to the publicity mill or just half-serious mind games is as unknowable as whether a given entertainer's spot on *Live Aid* was motivated by a simple wish to help the starving or an opportunity to either plug a record or simply prance around in front of the world. How could anyone ever tell?

In any case, the enigma of the sunshine and showers of Mick and Keith's friendship couldn't be formulated in plain terms any more than any long and intimate relationship, cemented by common ordeal and jubilation, that has endured from childhood to middle age. 'Mick's and my battles are not exactly as perceived through the press or other people,' elucidated Keith, 'They're far more convoluted – because we've known each other

KEITH RICHARDS

for most of our lives. So they involve more subtleties and ins and outs than could possibly be explained.'⁵

Over the next two years, there were periods when only the rare postcard filtered between Jagger and Richards. Other than these, they knew each other only by what was in the newspapers, the same as everyone else. Those within or on the periphery of the Stones' inner circle came to realise that, as it was with the messiest of divorces, you had to side with one or the other – though David Bowie was able to hedge his bets by duetting with Mick on 'Dancing In The Street', a charity single for the *Live Aid* relief fund, and seizing the opportunity to be photographed with Keith at some *après*-concert gathering for publication in the *New Musical Express*. The feeling was that, though Jagger was the most engaging and commercially operable of the two, Richards could produce some rabbit from the hat that would bring about his ascendancy.

As 1987 got under way, Jagger made a second album – *Primitive Cool* – without the other Stones. There were also reports of both a fire that necessitated total evacuation on the final day of sessions and, less specifically, intriguing sounds emitting from New York's then unfashionable Studio 900, one of the locations where Keith was recording his first *bona fide* solo album in accordance with a deal covering only him that he was about to wrap up with Virgin Records. Personnel were drawn mainly from The New Barbarians, the *Hail! Hail! Rock 'N' Roll* stage fixtures and *Dirty Work* auxiliaries, but more notable bit-part players were Mick Taylor, The Memphis Horns – derived from The Markeys, who'd preceded Booker T and the MGs as Stax's house band – and Bootsy Collins, former James Brown bass guitarist-turned-solo attraction.⁷

As it had been with *Dirty Work*, *Talk Is Cheap*'s 11 selections – co-written with Steve Jordan – were uninflated with gratuitous frills, and designed to be reproduced on the boards without much difficulty. The most contrived studio artifice was some backwards-running instrument fading in and out of the opening 'Big Enough', otherwise perhaps the most typical track with its murky deliberation and a snare drum almost as prominent as a lead vocal, like a Kentish cross between Bobs Dylan and Marley with a hint of post-war bluesman Slim Harpo.

Likewise, on 'Rockawhile' and 'Make No Mistake', Sarah Dash was as loud as Keith in what amounted to virtual duets. Yet, if she outclassed him technically, his inability to stray far beyond his central two octaves reinforced an idiosyncratic allure peculiar to certain singers who warp an intrinsically limited range and eccentric delivery to their own devices. In this oligarchy too are androgynous Adam Faith, wobbly David Bowie, frail Phil May, mesmerically ugly Bob Dylan and, of course, Mick Jagger. A Caruso-loving fly on the Studio 900 wall may well have blocked his ears, but, in context, Keith's efforts were not unattractive, even gruffly charming. At times, rather than try and fail to hit notes, he extemporised huskily like a soul man, as though a random couplet's sentiment couldn't be expressed through orthodox articulation.

Keith's controlled guitar solos and *obligatos* were less of a revelation. These were refreshingly straightforward when compared to other players' *de rigueur* reaction with face-contorting flash to underlying chord patterns rather than the more obvious aesthetics of a song. As far as I'm concerned, that puts Keith Richards in a *different* rather than *lower* league to Eric Clapton and his sort with their blisteringly high-velocity string-bending.

As a production – with Steve Jordan, who the sharp-eyed had spotted beating drums in *The Blues Brothers* movie – *Talk Is Cheap* was characterised by not so much uncalled-for soloing as 'laying down a groove' via repeated choruses and extended fades that put some in a hypnotic (or stoned) trance while others wondered, 'How much longer?' However, constant replay was necessary for details – such as the understated violin in downbeat 'Locked Away' and *sotto voce* muttering in 'Struggle' – to assume sharper focus.

Living only in riffs and perfunctory syllables strung together to carry a tune, some of the compositions worked less as separate entities than the summoning of atmospheres in which it was the rough-and-ready sound at any given moment that counted. 'I have more exact, more perfect or skilful takes of each of the songs,' said Richards before reiterating the old mantra, 'The more you try to literally perfect them, the more you lose the instinctive thing. Instinct is what I want.'[5]

Much of *Talk Is Cheap* was maddeningly, and probably unavoidably, familiar – a 'Street Fighting Man'-ish *ostinato* here, a Bo Diddley inflection there, vamping Chuck Berry-like piano triplets (courtesy of Johnnie Johnson) elsewhere. Ample helpings of dub-reggae, Cajun-Zydeco, Buddy Holly and the Crickets-like backing chorale (in 'I Could Have Stood You Up'), *Missa Luba* jungle mass and James Brown tension-building were served up too. 'Big Enough' wouldn't have been out of place on a Police album – and, by Keith's own admission, The Beatles surfaced somehow in 'Whip It Up'.

Yet an inbred originality rode roughshod over all the stylistic borrowing and, while Frank Sinatra, jackpot of all songwriters, was unlikely to cover them, certain compositions *per se* could be reduced most serviceably to the acid test of just voice and piano, overtly the 'Take It So Hard' and 'Make No Mistake' singles and, catchier still, 'You Don't Move Me', a supposed swipe at Jagger, spelt out in its *diminuendo* coda.

Two could play at Jagger's game, and in the same month as the final date of Mick's jaunt Down Under in November 1988, Keith embarked on a fortnight of engagements across the States with The X-Pensive Winos, an amalgam of the less illustrious *Talk Is Cheap* assistants. As well as the album *in toto*, they gave 'em 'Happy', 'Time Is On My Side' (featuring Sarah Dash) and, most bygone of all, 'Connection' from the Stones canon plus

'Run Rudolph Run' – which became more and more fitting as the tour crept nearer to its climax a week before Christmas Day in New Jersey in front of a crowd over 20,000 strong.

This had been heralded by a publicity blitz conspicuous for a spot on *Smile Jamaica*, a concert in London for victims of an unforeseen hurricane that had damaged properties – including Point Of View – throughout the island. Patiently puffing a perpetual cigarette, Richards also gave unblinking offstage copy, frequently tormenting questioners with hints of a Stones comeback.

This wasn't as mischievous as it seemed, because the parts hadn't equalled the whole. Of all the non-Stones ventures, Mick's had, as predicted, been the most saleable, albeit on a law of diminishing returns – though figures for *Talk Is Cheap* had been healthy enough for moderate placings in Top 40s across the globe.

Furthermore, time had healed and there lingered memories of the struggle back in 1962 and its fantastic outcome when, on 18 May 1988 at the Savoy in London, Richards, Wyman, Watts and Jagger with Ron Wood met together for the first time in two years. After loosening up with selective reminiscences, it was agreed that the only barriers to picking up where they'd left off in 1986 were outstanding extra-curricular commitments and what Keith referred to as the 'family squabble. If I shout and scream at him, it's because no-one else has the guts to do it.'[8]

Richards and Jagger each kept civil tongues in their heads over a drink in New York three months later when they decided to rent a house near Eddy Grant's studio in Barbados – neutral territory between Jamaica and Mick's spread in Mustique – to see how full the Jagger–Richards creative well could be, and whether they could bear to be on the same lump of plastic as each other again. As Patti waved him off, Keith told her to expect him back in either two days or two months 'because I'll know within forty-eight hours whether this thing is going to work or if we are just going to be catting and dogging.'[9]

Mixing business with pleasure in Barbados, the Wentworth Primary old boys 'used to go out to the clubs every night. Keith sat at the bar drinking, and I went on the dance floor. Keith doesn't like to dance. He's too shy. He doesn't really verbally communicate.'[10]

An obtuse speculation is that, if in some parallel dimension, this working holiday hadn't ended with sufficient new songs for an album – and the writers' reignited enthusiasm for the Stones – the market void might have been filled by one of any number of groups in the same image, 'with one of me in each of them', added Keith.[11] With The New York Dolls long gone, chief among leading contenders were The Black Crowes, a laddish bunch from Atlanta with a bar-room blues style, reprobate image and, well, crowe's-nest haircuts. It was through Richards' recommendation that bass player Greg Rzeb from John Mayall's Bluesbreakers became a Black Crowe when a vacancy arose. Keith felt less benevolence towards Manchester's Stone Roses, who all but plagiarised The Rolling Stones' name almost as surely as any of the tribute bands – The Rollin' Stoned, The Rolling Clones, The Strolling Ones *ad nauseum* – that were emerging in the late 1980s.

Doris Richards was, reputedly, a fan of The Rollin' Stoned, but Keith seemed bemused generally that anyone should make a living impersonating the Stones. More interesting to him was a contemporaneous garage band scene that was spreading as a global cult. Form was determined by the phonographic equivalent of bottling lightning in youthful (or not-so-youthful) adrenaline with thrilling margins of error pumped onto a spool of tape – while content mingled overhauls of genre artefacts with riff-based (and often derivative) originals, executed with a rough-hewn verve. Steeped in 1960s beat boom music and attitude – and often recorded in defiantly anachronistic mono – The Diaboliks, The Thanes, The Thunderbyrds, The Inmates, The Dukes Of Hamburg and *Thee* Headcoats were among

British brand leaders, with the latter amalgamating with The Downliners Sect for a long player entitled *Deerstalking Men*, and bossing a Medway towns scene that was as self-contained in its way as it had been during the era of Bern Elliott, Terry Lee and Erkey Grant.

While the Stones weren't to tread the backwards path as much as Thee Headcoats, the exhilaration of spontaneity was prized more than accuracy during the five weeks in the West Indies needed to record 1989's *Steel Wheels*, 'the meanest rock 'n' roll machine to hit the streets this summer', glowed the *New Musical Express*.[12] As well as including 'Almost Hear You Sigh', penned by Richards and Jordan in 1987, it could have been Keith talking about *Talk Is Cheap*, when, at the press conference at Grand Central Station to launch the *Steel Wheels* tour, Mick averred, 'Yes, a lot of it sounds really garagey. We didn't want it to sound too tidy, so we just followed our initial instincts.'[12]

18 The Main Offender

'Surprisingly, Keith Richards is the most attentive husband and father, very dedicated to his family.'
– Dorothy Stein (tour masseuse) [1]

On any Tuesday throughout most of the mid-1980s, The Pretty Things – with only Phil May and Dick Taylor left from the original Sidcup Art College group – were knocking 'em dead in an auditorium above a fashionable Little Venice pub. For 50 pence admission, an astonishing young clientele would witness a laid-back joviality in place of 1965's scowls, and guest performers of such diversity as Ian Stewart, Mick Avory of The Kinks, Glen Matlock and Bruce Brand from Thee Headcoats.

The Things' return to contemporary prominence culminated in October 2002 with a sensational exhumation of *SF Sorrow* at the Royal Festival Hall. However, for Dick Taylor, it was the Festival Hall today and ambling to the newsagents tomorrow – as if he'd never won that acclaim as a Pretty Thing or loomed large in the legend of The Rolling Stones. Yet, he is attractive in his phlegmatic candour. Rather than bitterness at missing the millions he might have accrued had he gone the distance with Keith and Mick – with whom he has remained in touch – he reflects that he may, alternatively, have gone the way of poor Brian Jones.

Conversely, he might have been an unlikely Judy Garland of pop like Keith now that Richards was no longer a human rag crossing a terrible desert with an empty canteen, buoyed by a drug-begotten and surreal mirage of a rescue ship surging through the scorching rocks and flesh-lacerating cacti. Awaiting him on the other side in the first instance was morbid inquisitiveness from those who looked and wondered. Onstage was not a common-or-garden pop star, but a man who'd been to hell and back. Others cognisant with Richards' personal vulnerability and turbulent life worried when he seemed to flag, cheered when he recovered and glowed when his lead vocal spot went down especially well. Rather than 'Happy', this tended to be 'Before They Make Me Run', 'Little T & A' from *Tattoo You* – also quasi-autobiographical (as exemplified by its observation that pushers were disgruntled because he was no longer interested in hard drugs) – or, later, 'The Worst' from 1994's *Voodoo Lounge*.

Every day Keith still lived was a bonus. Whatever had been wrong was righting itself now that most of the mainly self-invoked devils had been sweated from him, even if he continued to play up to an old image. At some awards ceremony or other of the many he attended nowadays as both presenter and nominee, Richards was sober and coherent at his table, but, like the late Oliver Reed, his opposite number in the world of drama, he pretended to be real, real gone when called to the podium – cosmetic fish-hooks and amulets dangling from his hair: dear, old Keith, drunk before breakfast, stoned before lunch time...

Yet it had been noted that he was imbibing mineral water in preference to his off-duty vodka-with-orange soda when back at Studio 900 in August 1992 to record a second solo album, *Main Offender*. Its making was a reflection of not internal dissent in the Stones anymore, but a more mature attitude. They were now not so much a group, see, as perhaps an artistic *kolkhoz* in which members could plough this or that extra-mural furrow with the blessing of the rest – unless, of course, they considered that it threatened direct rivalry to the integral unit. This was to extend as far as Keith headlining a concert on behalf of the Rain Forest

Alliance at New York's Beacon Theatre – where he was lauded by compere Jackson Browne as 'one of the finest singer-songwriters of our time' – though there had been little evidence of this on *Main Offender*.

Completed with, more or less, the *Talk Is Cheap* personnel in attendance, *Main Offender* was hailed by younger critics for whom it was given that Keith *was* The Rolling Stones, but was otherwise deemed unexciting – certainly not as ear-catching as *Talk Is Cheap*. Repeated spins put individual tracks – notably '999', 'Eileen' and the soulful 'Demon' – in sharper focus, but nothing screamed out as a blatant single that might or might not irritate the Top 50, let alone be an unmistakable 'Happy'-like smash. The most fundamental flaws were the dragging out of songs – with 'Words Of Wonder' almost touching the seven-minute mark – to a greater degree than *Talk Is Cheap*, and certain lyrics that may have contained opaque gems of worldly wisdom, but were more likely just words to sing.

To be brutal, *Main Offender* was much of a muchness, though the playing and production was proficient, and Keith, within his limits, in fine voice. Yet who the hell am I to criticise an album that spread itself thinly enough over a long period to sell moderately well while dithering on the edge of the charts in both Britain and the States?

No one could moan either that Keith had let the album fend for itself. Its promotion included X-Pensive Winos shows in Argentina, a short European tour – that took in an engagement at the Marquee – and some US showcases, notably two numbers at the first International Rock Awards televised from New York's Armory[2] where Eric Clapton handed Richards an award – a 12-inch statuette of Elvis Presley – for being a 'Living Legend'.

Keith also submitted to a signing session at Tower Records in New York, which sucked in a crowd of over 3,000; making himself pleasant at *Rolling Stone* magazine's 25th anniversary party in one of the city's restaurants, and speaking to *Kerrang*, a chief mouthpiece of heavy metal (in which he dismissed fame as 'a mind-rotting thing').[3]

In the beginning, he'd scarcely been able to say boo to a goose, but these days, Keith Richards was becoming known in the media as a great talker, answering inquisitors with unblinking self-assurance and carefully honed intellectual self-defence: plain speaking laced with quirky wit that didn't always sound so funny in print as in his lazy Korner-esque manner while slouched in a chair. The way he told 'em was more important than the quotes themselves. Here are some that have stood the test of time:

'I would rather be a living legend than a dead legend.'[4]

'There was really just one song ever written, and that was by Adam and Eve. We just do the variations.'[5]

'Like I said many years ago, I've never had a problem with drugs, only with cops.'[4]

'I don't look to go through life being someone else's image of Keith Richards. I know who he is. I'm inside him. The idea of partying for nine days in order to keep the image of Keith Richards up is stupid. That was Keith Richards then. Now I'll stay up just two or three days.'[6]

'Being famous is OK, but in the courtroom, it works against you.'[4]

Not quite vintage Richards, however, was a bald, 'You try living out of a suitcase for twenty years.'[7] He compared himself to 'a whaling captain' in that 'the most I've spent in one place is three months. It's hello and goodbye.'[8] He'd let go of 3 Cheyne Walk, and Redlands had been out of commission again after a second fire. This time, agitated oscillations brought 65 firemen, sufficient to ensure that the only serious damage was to the roof. More niggling than heartsinking, however, were fraught if discreet discussions between Keith and the local council about the redirection of a public cycle path passing within yards of the place.

As well as Sussex, Keith and Patti dwelt in Jamaica, Paris, deep in leafy Connecticut and, as a New York pied-à-terre, a loft conversion along Lower Broadway, which was insulated against complaints about loud records, just as Keith's hotel rooms were, whenever possible, to minimise annoyance to other guests.

Accepting that there were perks in consanguineous complexities, all sub-divisions of kindred flitted to and from the various locations in harmony. 'My kids are the straightest in the world,' grinned Keith, illustrating this with Angela's teetotalism, although 'Marlon likes a drop of champagne now and then'. [4]

After more academically successful years at art school than his sire, Marlon had found employment as a road manager for the latter-day Who – fixed solely on their back catalogue – prior to founding the art collective Zoltar The Magnificent. By 2003, he was creative co-ordinator of New York periodical *Cheap Date*. This, he said, comes out 'whenever we have enough money'. [9] He was, by now, also father of two, having married a Lucie de la Falaise nine years earlier.

In the midst of a North American tour with the Stones, Keith couldn't make the ceremony in Italy, and was represented by Patti. Nonetheless, he walked Angela down the aisle – to the pipe-organ strains of the Stones' 30-year-old ballad 'Angie', rather than the traditional 'Wedding March' – when she wed carpenter Dominic Jennings. They settled in Dartford where the bride was still involved in equestrian matters, teaching children to ride.

Angela and Marlon would be present at Keith's star-studded 50th birthday celebrations at New York's plush Metropole Restaurant, but, as they jetted overhead, their mother was standing in a supermarket checkout queue less than an hour away from Dartford (via the commuter line to Victoria). In 1990, 48-year-old Anita Pallenberg had enrolled as a mature student for a degree course in textiles and fashion at Central St Martin's Design School,[10] bicycling to class through what little remained of the Swinging Sixties from her home off King's Road. Now as much 'into' exercise as she was heroin, Anita was down to eight stones. She wasn't quite as wasp-waisted, but still comfortably trim in spring 2004 when sharing the proverbial joke with one of Mick's daughters at the opening night of the 'Vivienne Westwood' exhibition at the Victoria and Albert Museum. Her gleaming and suspiciously even teeth seemed to have a good few bites left in them.

Anita is on cordial terms with her children's stepsisters. With Leah, Ron Wood's daughter, Theodora and Alexandra thrust their heads above the parapet when instrumental in the launch of the Stones' designer range, Fashion And Licks; Theodora going so far as to make a debut as a model in US *Vogue* in 2002 – while less glossy media organs attempted to make a dynastic marriage of James Jagger, Mick's eldest son, dating Alexandra for a while.

The paternal grandparents, Bert and Doris, had seen each other for the first time in decades at Keith's nuptials. At the table head during the reception, he may have eyed them, wondering if a dam would burst on an eventual outpouring of home truths or if the abyss would ever be bridged.[11]

As if watching a tennis match too, Bill, Charlie and Ron had flickered from Keith to Mick as the differences between them had resolved. 'They're like brothers,' opined Watts, 'always arguing, but always getting on.'[12] A residue of tension, however, may have spiced up performances during the *Steel Wheels* world tour. It was the biggest-grossing such enterprise in history. Even the now regular strategy of fitting in an appearance at a small venue was magnified by a webcast audience of three million via a deal with a pay-by-view cable TV company.

Arrests, riots and general mayhem belonged to the past –
though the Chinese government weren't so certain. Reasons for
the break-down of lengthy negotiations for a Stones maiden
appearance in Beijing were summarised in a letter that alighted on
Keith's doormat. 'Number One on the list is "Cultural
Pollution",' he sneered, 'and about Number Thirty is "Will cause
traffic jams" – and in between is a whole load of other crap.' [13]

Yet the most far-reaching mishap this time round was
Richards pricking a finger on the needle-like end of a string on
the customised Telecaster nicknamed 'Micawber', and the
consequent infection forcing the rescheduling of dates at Cardiff
Arms Park and Wembley.

Occurrences of more insidious occupational hazards, however,
were much reduced now that Keith had braked his erratic
timekeeping. His persevering with relative abstention also had a
beneficial effect on the music. 'With Keith sober, the Stones now
are playing better than I've ever heard them,' smiled Arnold Dunn,
adding, nonetheless, that 'Keith usually has a little party-ette with
a few friends in his room until about seven in the morning. He
doesn't sleep like you or I do. He just lies down on the sofa and
crashes out for four or five hours when he feels the need.' [14]

A mere road manager said one thing, Bill Wyman said
another. 'Keith doesn't play very well,' he told a US radio
presenter in February 1991. Such waspishness – as both his
target and Bill himself realised – could be laughed off just as
Keith's and Mick's derogatory remarks about each other had
been during the mid-1980s stand-off. Nevertheless, Wyman was
no longer bothered about, say, having to learn parrot-fashion the
bass lines that Keith – the self-styled 'benevolent tyrant' [15] behind
the closed doors of the studio – had played on this or that track
on the latest album, *Flashpoint*. He also had more crucial
business on his mind than turning up for the video shoot near
Brooklyn Bridge for a spin-off single, 'Highwire'. Nearing his
60s, Wyman's retirement was now an *idée fixe*.

'Bill bowed out gracefully because he couldn't guarantee that 100% anymore' was Keith's rationale[15] as the Stones accustomed themselves to life without him – and with a substitute bass player for the tour that tied in with the release of 1994's *Voodoo Lounge*. The transition enacted, it seemed as if no harm had been done what with 60,000 packing out Washington's RFK Stadium to clap almost-but-not-quite as hard for two items from *Voodoo Lounge* and three from *Exile On Main Street* as for 'Not Fade Away', 'Satisfaction' and a 'Honky Tonk Women' accompanied by a video of female icons from Shirley Temple to Elizabeth Taylor on a monster screen. *In toto*, it was, gasped *USA Today*, 'a battering ram of a show that finds the Stones rock 'n' rolling like hellions on wheels. Unlike Pink Floyd members, who are cardboard stiffs amid an awesome array of lasers and lights, the Stones are lively and watchable, capable of competing with the non-stop cyberworld stimuli.'[16]

Yet, if each stadium stop had to be powered by over three million watts of power and eight miles of cable, the tour's most appealing souvenir was *Stripped*, the nearest the Stones had ever come to a then-trendy 'unplugged' album, taped largely during pre-concert rehearsals and soundchecking. 'We're as accustomed to playing acoustic as we are electric,' elucidated Keith, 'It's not just learning the songs or deciding which ones to play. It's the process of welding together. There's no pressure on you. It's all, "Play this. Try this. Try that" – like brainstorming sessions. That's the kind of feeling I wanted.'[17]

While it was by no means entirely acoustic, there was a neo-downhome ambience about the endearing and relaxed overhauls of blues throwbacks to the Craw Daddy, near-forgotten B-sides and fourth-track-side-twos of LPs plus 'Angie', 'Street Fighting Man' and nothing else that could be dated past the early 1970s, apart from 'Slipping Away', a minor *Steel Wheels* item with Keith as lead singer – and who could not derive vicarious delight from the Stones piling into Bob Dylan's 'Like A Rolling Stone' at London's Brixton Academy?

Keith had developed quite a taste for such re-investigations. Before *Stripped*, he'd assisted George Jones on the grizzled and hard-drinking C&W star's re-recordings of his genre hits in Nashville. In the same bag was Keith's rendition of 'You Win Again' on *Timeless*, a Hank Williams tribute collection. He'd also completed another circle by paying contributory respects to Elvis Presley on *All The King's Men* – produced under the aegis of Scotty Moore and drummer DJ Fontana – and felt as honoured when invited to play too on albums by Johnnie Johnson[18] and John Lee Hooker.

By no means confined to olde-tyme behemoths of country, blues and classic rock, he would brush up his reggae with Toots And The Maytals, The Skatalites and, on his own Mindless record label, *Wingless Angels* with some Rastafarians local to Point Of View. He had also supplied a melody to 'That Feel' for 1992's raw *Bone Machine* by chin-bearded post-beatnik Tom Waits.

Richards allowed himself too a more pronounced stake in charitable proceedings. Six weeks after 9/11 – when hijacked aeroplanes had torn into New York's World Trade Centre – he and Mick gave 'em 'Salt Of The Earth' (from *Beggars Banquet*) and 'Miss You' when among Billy Idol, Destiny's Child, The Who, Paul McCartney, Bon Jovi, David Bowie and the rest of the artistes who did their bit at Madison Square Garden to show solidarity against terrorism, and raise money for firefighters and victims.

This event could not be seized upon as an unforeseeable but welcome opportunity to trumpet any fresh Stones merchandise then. Neither was there any in the shops – unless you counted a remixed 'Sympathy For The Devil' single – when, beginning in 2003, the group entertained three million on yet another world tour. Concentrating on the possible, they'd defined their motivations sharply enough: to become a showbusiness institution; for the marketing problems of age, obesity and baldness that dog others of similar vintage not to matter, and to not need to justify the words of John McNally of a still-functioning 'official' Searchers: 'You don't have to be young to make good records.'[19]

A current chart entry would have been pleasant but non-essential for the Stones. The same was true of Chuck Berry, who thrived more integrally on his past both on the boards and via the royalties that others were earning for him – most recently via 'Schooldays' by Ann Rabson, a Philadelphia-based singing barrelhouse pianist, who won't ever be as immortal as Ma Rainey or Big Mama Thornton.

Rabson's revival generated mere pin-money compared to what the Stones might have amassed for Berry. Yet, while Keith was reputed to spin a ritual Berry track in the dressing room just prior to venturing onstage, since *Hail! Hail! Rock 'N' Roll* – and the later issue of *Sweet Little Sexteen*, an 80-minute video featuring old Chuck in manifold sexual activities – they'd been less inclined to insert Berry numbers into the set.

However disillusioned he may have been about his boyhood hero's lack of dignity, Keith was more vocal about the knighting of Mick Jagger in 2004 on Prime Minister Tony Blair's vote-catching advice. To Richards' belittling of the investiture in the left-wing *Guardian* – as 'a paltry honour from the same establishment that did their very best to throw us in jail and kill us',[12] – Jagger had retorted in *The Times*, 'He likes to make a bit of a fuss. He would probably like the same honour himself. Keith's like a bawling child who hasn't got an ice cream.'[20]

My own feeling is that if Jagger was to be so exalted, the other Stones deserved to be too, just as all four Beatles had when decorated with their MBEs in 1966. If that had been the case, how willingly would Keith Richards have been to be driven through the cheering crowds to Buckingham Palace? How would it have affected his standing as the Stones' resident loveable scamp and chain-smoking, pool-shooting everyman? Meeting Richards in the customs queue at Heathrow Airport, Chrissie Hynde of The Pretenders would remember, 'We walked to the gate together, and it was extraordinary the amount of people who passed him and said, "Hey Keith, how're you doing, mate?". They certainly wouldn't have done it if it was Mick.'[12]

Epilogue
The Greying Eminence

'I get paid while I sleep.' – *Keith Richards*[1]

What is Keith doing at this moment? He probably isn't at the wheel of a car as he tends not to drive anymore. If he's tucking into a meal, it's likely to contain meat as he's non-vegetarian with a particular fondness for pork sausages laced with leek and ginger.

With a cigarette at his lips, maybe he's trancing out to a favoured heavy metal band like AC/DC – or to classical music, detested until he 'realised there's quite a lot going on there. If only Mozart had had a good drummer... Music is the only thing that interests me apart from reading.'[2]

Learning from them in his own special way, the tomes on Keith Richards' bookshelf reveal a wide, omnivorous and erratic taste – biographies of Miles Davis and Thelonius Monk, a treatise about herbal remedies, military history, Dostoevsky, Raymond Chandler...

So we leave the pain-free old age of one perhaps torn between tears and relief. Now able to be waited on, hand and foot, for all the years left to him, all he needs to do is sit back and let the royalties continue to roll in. At any given moment, a radio or television station somewhere in the world is airing a Jagger–Richards composition by either the Stones or via one of shoals of cover versions. Only a few weeks ago, 'Ruby Tuesday' was sung *omnes fortissimo* during an episode of BBC 1's *Cutting It* drama series.

Other Stones' A-sides – and the better-known album tracks – have lasted well too. Nevertheless, watching an edition of the now-ailing *Top of The Pops* often begs the question: who wants proper songs anymore – least of all ones with the class of 'Satisfaction', 'Sympathy For The Devil', 'Wild Horses', even 1981's 'Start Me Up'? The increasingly more lost value of someone singing a song as opposed to producing a production could indicate the impending end of pop itself – or, at least, the sort of pop I loved – the sort of pop that ruled the airwaves in my 1960s adolescence.

To paraphrase Mandy Rice-Davies, I would say that, wouldn't I? If ever you catch me in full philistine flood, moaning and sour-graping about pop music these days, it'll be like hearing my dad going on about The Rolling Stones in 1964. Yet even he would admit that, while he thought they were rubbish, at least they were British rubbish. It's doubtful whether such an opinion matters to him but, if it does, Keith Richards, once a self-confessed 'layabout' and now one of the richest men in Britain, can die easy.

Notes

In addition to my own correspondence and interviews, I have used the following sources, which I would like to credit:

Prologue: Mr Showbusiness

1 *Keith Richards In His Own Words* ed. M St Michael (Omnibus, 1994)
2 *Loose Talk* ed. L Botts (Rolling Stone Press, 1980)
3 *Q*, October 1988
4 *Rolling Stones In Their Own Words* ed. D Dalton and M Farren (Omnibus, 1985)

Chapter 1: The Kentish Man

1 *Telling The Teenagers: A Guide For Parents, Teachers And Youth Leaders* by Rose Hacker (Andre Deutsch, 1957)
2 Sleeve notes to *Hoochie Coochie Men: A History Of British Blues And R&B, 1955–2001* by various artists (Indigo IGBX 2501, 2002)
3 *Q*, November 1992
4 *Keith Richards In His Own Words* ed. M St Michael (Omnibus, 1994)
5 *Everybody's Weekly*, 3 July 1957
6 *The Guardian*, 5 September 2003
7 *Rolling Stones In Their Own Words* ed. D Dalton and M Farren (Omnibus, 1985)
8 I'm not certain whether the plural of Elvis should be Elv*i* or the second declension Elv*es*. What do you think?
9 *Q*, October 1988
10 *Streets Of London: The Official Biography Of Ralph McTell* by C Hockenhull (Northdown, 1997) Today, in many folk clubs, it's a rare evening that passes without some seated twerp with a guitar emoting the 'Johnny B Goode' of the genre, McTell's 'Streets Of London'.

Chapter 2: The Art Student

1   *The Guardian*, a Tuesday in 1996 (precise date obscured)

2   *Melody Maker*, 8 January 1962

3   *Blues Guitar* ed. J Obrecht (Miller Freeman, 1993) Eventually, Keith would own copies of Johnson's two death certificates – each with a contradictory statement about how he perished.

4   *The Rolling Stones As It Happened: The Classic Interviews* (Chrome Dreams CIS 2002/1, 2001)

5   *New Musical Express*, 8 May 1964

Chapter 3: The Fellow Traveller

1   *Hoochie Coochie Men: A History Of British Blues And R&B, 1955–2001* by various artists (Indigo IGBX 2501, 2002)

2   This tape was to fetch just over £50,000 at a Sotheby's auction in 1995.

3   *Blues Guitar* ed. J Obrecht (Miller Freeman, 1993)

4   One of few versions I've ever heard on which you could make out all the words.

5   *Keith Richards In His Own Words* ed. M St Michael (Omnibus, 1994)

6   *Jazz News*, 11 July 1962

7   He was to rename himself Alvin *Lee* when a member of Ten Years After.

8   *The Sunday Times*, 10 August 2003

9   *Jeff Beck: Crazy Fingers* by A Carson (Carson, 1998)

10 *Q*, October 1988

Chapter 4: Cliff's Brother

1   *Keith Richards In His Own Words* ed. M St Michael (Omnibus, 1994)

2   Founded nine years earlier by trumpeter Ken Colyer as what he recognised as a 'home of purist traditional jazz' (*London Live* by T Bacon [Balafon, 1999]). Now, however, it had a new guideline that enabled trad bands and the likes of the Stones, The Downliners Sect and The Yardbirds to share the same bill.

3   *The Sunday Times*, 13 November 1966

4   *Q*, October 1988

5   *New Musical Express*, 4 September 1964

6   Keith Richards himself ratified the official restoration of the 's' via an EMI memo in the mid-1970s – though it had long been printed on composing credits and elsewhere on record packaging.

7   *Stoned: A Memoir of London in the 1960s* by AL Oldham (St Martin's Press, 2001)

8   *Melody Maker*, 26 September 1964

9   *Q*, May 1995

10 *New York Times*, 20 December 1964

11 *Rolling Stone*, 5 November 1987

12 *Rolling Stones In Their Own Words* ed. D Dalton and M Farren (Omnibus, 1985)

13 *The Life And Times Of Little Richard: The Quasar Of Rock* by C White (Pan, 1985)

14 *Who's Who In Popular Music* ed. S Tracy (World's Work, 1984)

15 *New Musical Express*, 2 August 1963

16 *New Musical Express*, 27 November 1964

Chapter 5: The Anti-Beatle

1 *The Real Buddy Holly Story* by E Amburn (Virgin, 1996)

2 *Revolution In The Head* by I Macdonald (Pimlico, 1995)

3 *Q*, October 1988

4 A remarkable revival of this twist-in-the-tale opus by British singing guitarist Graham Larkbey was released as a single in the mid-1980s.

5 That in turn drew upon a pre-war blues by Memphis Minnie.

6 *Rolling Stones In Their Own Words* ed. D Dalton and M Farren (Omnibus, 1985)

7 *Herald Of Wales*, July 1964

8 *Ptolemaic Terrascope*, May 1990

9 *Keith Richards In His Own Words* ed. M St Michael (Omnibus, 1994)

Chapter 6: The Fuzz Boxer

1 *Rolling Stone*, 5 November 1987

2 *Travelling Man* by F Allen (Aureus, 1999)

3 *Rolling Stones In Their Own Words* ed. D Dalton and M Farren (Omnibus, 1985)

4 *We Gotta Go Now* by DA Blackledge (Windholme, 1998)

5 *Keith Richards In His Own Words* ed. M St Michael (Omnibus, 1994)

6 *Billboard*, February 1964

7 As well as 'My Girl', the Stones themselves recorded three more items associated with Redding: 'Pain In My Heart', 'That's How Strong My Love Is' and 'I've Been Loving You Too Long'.

8 Among multitudinous versions are those by Manfred Mann, Mary Wells, Billy Preston, Sandie Shaw, Chris Farlowe, Jose Feliciano, Blue Cheer, Bubblerock (alias Jonathan King), Aretha Franklin, The Troggs, Devo and Samantha Fox. In 1968, a certain Paraffin Jack Flash Ltd would issue an instrumental 'Satisfaction', but this was nowhere as so-bad-it's-good as a revival by the incomparable Portsmouth Sinfonia in 1979. Most recently, an all-but-unrecognisable version was released in 2004 by Charlie Watts' 11-piece jazz combo

9   *Behind The Song* by M Heatley and S Leigh (Blandford, 1998)

10 *New Musical Express*, 3 September 1965

11 Further endorsements would come from The Beatles, who fed a bass guitar through one when preparing their winter album, *Rubber Soul*, and it was also to electroplate 'Keep On Running' and 'Somebody Help Me', consecutive 1966 British chart-toppers for The Spencer Davis Group, as well as late-1965's 'You Make It Move' and the 'Hold Tight!' follow-up by Dave, Dee, Dozy, Beaky, Mick and Tich.

12 *Daily Mail*, 19 July 1990

13 *Faithfull* by M Faithfull and D Dalton (Penguin, 1995) However, I must add the raw information that Keith wrote the 1967 Stones A-side 'Let's Spend The Night Together' on the piano. 'Let's Spend The Night Together' was recorded by Muddy Waters in 1969.

14 *New Musical Express*, 23 September 1966

15 This third single by The Game – from Mitcham, Surrey – was released on Parlophone in 1967, but deleted soon afterwards.

Chapter 7: Prisoner No. 7855

1   *Daily Mail*, 18 July 1990

2   Namely, 'The Last Time', 'Play With Fire', 'Mother's Little Helper', 'Take It Or Leave It' and 'Sittin' On A Fence'. *À propos* nothing in particular, Richard Ashcroft of The Verve was to sample the Aranbee Pop Symphony Orchestra's version of 'The Last Time' for the introit to 1997's 'Bitter Sweet Symphony'.

3   Who had appropriated as a visual trademark a 'windmill' guitar pose he'd noticed Keith employing onstage once in 1964.

4   *The Correspondent*, 11 February 1990

5   *The Yardbirds* by A Clayson (Backbeat, 2002)

6   *Loose Talk* ed. L Botts (Rolling Stone Press, 1980)

7   *The Sunday Times*, 2 May 2004

8   *Faithfull* by M Faithfull and D Dalton (Penguin, 1995)

9   *Rolling Stones In Their Own Words* ed. D Dalton and M Farren (Omnibus, 1985)

10 *Daily Express*, 5 November 1987

11 To Jan Wenner

12 *International Times*, 11 September 1969

13 *International Times*, 17 May 1967

14 *Self-Portrait With Friends: The Selected Diaries of Cecil Beaton 1926–1974* ed. R Buckle (Book Club Associates, 1980)

15 *The Rolling Stones As It Happened: The Classic Interviews* (Chrome Dreams CIS 2002/1, 2001)

Chapter 8: His Satanic Majesty

1   *The Sunday Times*, 17 August 2003
2   *Q*, October 1988
3   *The Lamberts* by A Motion (Chatto and Windus, 1986)
4   *Keith Richards In His Own Words* ed. M St Michael (Omnibus, 1994)
5   *Neil's Book Of The Dead* by N Planer and T Blacker (Pavilion, 1984)
6   *International Times*, 17 May 1967
7   *Loose Talk* ed. L Botts (Rolling Stone Press, 1980)
8   *New Musical Express*, 9 December 1969

Chapter 9: The Demon Brother

1   *The Sunday Times*, 6 January 1991
2   *New Musical Express*, 9 August 1969
3   *Rock: The Rough Guide* ed. J Buckley and M Ellington (Rough Guides, 1996)
4   *Blues In Britain* by B Brunning (Blandford, 1995)
5   Which, if accepted by the Home Office as a legal marriage, might have quelled intense and unwelcome interest in Anita's brittle status as a UK resident then.
6   *Keith Richards In His Own Words* ed. M St Michael (Omnibus, 1994)
7   *Q*, October 1988
8   *Shattered*, Issue 19, 20 June 2000
9   *Rolling Stones In Their Own Words* ed. D Dalton and M Farren (Omnibus, 1985)

Chapter 10: The Wild Horseman

1   *Keith Richards In His Own Words* ed. M St Michael (Omnibus, 1994)
2   *Johnny Cash: The Last Great American*, BBC 1, 27 February 2004.
3   *The Rolling Stones Chronicle* by M Bonanno (Plexus, 1995)
4   *The Guardian*, 5 September 2003   There have been suggestions that Parsons may have co-written or, at least, inspired 'Torn And Frayed' and 'Sweet Virginia', C&W-tinged songs attributed to Richards and Jagger, and selected for 1972's *Exile On Main Street*.
5   *Back In The High Life* by A Clayson (Sidgwick and Jackson, 1988)
6   *Daily Mail*, 18 July 1990

Chapter 11: An Englishman Abroad

1   *Keith Richards In His Own Words* ed. M St Michael (Omnibus, 1994)
2   *Daily Mail*, 18 July 1990
3   So named after the original title, *Tropical Disease*, was jettisoned.

4   And so, apparently, was an album by singing actress Barbra Streisand.

5   *Blues Guitar* ed. J Obrecht (Miller Freeman, 1993)

6   *Rolling Stone Record Guide* ed. D Marsh and J Swenson (Virgin, 1980)

7   *Arena*, BBC 2, 27 November 1989

8   *Rolling Stones In Their Own Words* ed. D Dalton and M Farren (Omnibus, 1985)

9   Not the British group of the same name, whose best-remembered release was the 1963 single 'Come On Baby', a rocked-up adaptation of the Cornish Floral Dance.

10 *The Rolling Stones Chronicle* by M Bonanno (Plexus, 1995)

11 *Melody Maker*, 23 December 1974

12 *The Q/Omnibus Press Rock 'N' Roll Reader* ed. D Marsh (Q/Omnibus, 1994)

13 *The Correspondent*, 11 February 1990

Chapter 12: The Addicted Man

1   *Keith Richards In His Own Words* ed. M St Michael (Omnibus, 1994)

2   *Goldmine*, September 1981

3   *Melody Maker*, 6 September 1975

4   *Bob Marley* by S Davies (Granada, 1984)

5   *Loose Talk* ed. L Botts (Rolling Stone Press, 1980)

6   Though he was less flippant in a contemporaneous confession – which echoed Frank Zappa's comment – that 'they might have flashed the inspiration for a couple of good songs, but I don't think there's anything fantastic been written under the influence of drugs that couldn't have been written without.' (*Melody Maker*, 23 December 1974)

7   *The Guardian*, 5 September 2003

8   *The Sunday Times*, 14 September 2003

9   On Bastille Day that same year, Parsons' fellow ex-Byrd, Clarence White, had been unloading a station wagon outside his California home when another vehicle killed him instantly.

10 *The Guardian*, 6 February 2004

11 *The Times*, 6 March 2004.

12 *The Rolling Stones Chronicle* by M Bonanno (Plexus, 1995)

13 *Q*, October 1988

14 *The Rolling Stones As It Happened: The Classic Interviews* (Chrome Dreams CIS 2002/1, 2001)

15 *New Musical Express*, 27 July 1974

16 The elder Righteous Brother, Bobby Hatfield, passed away in 2003

17 Though Ian Stewart qualified this with, 'Keith is the leader of the band until such time that Mick will walk into a studio with a song he's written and

finished. If it's Mick's song, and it's stuck in his head how it's going to be, it'll be done usually.' (*Keith Richards In His Own Words* ed. M St Michael (Omnibus, 1994))

Chapter 13: The Zigzag Wanderer

1   *Melody Maker*, 23 December 1974

2   Four years earlier, Korner's CCS big band had released a version of 'Satisfaction' and, in 1980, an acoustic 'Honky Tonk Women' would be selected for *Me*, an Alexis Korner album that was issued only in Germany.

3   *Rolling Stones In Their Own Words* ed. D Dalton and M Farren (Omnibus, 1985)

4   *The Yardbirds* by A Clayson (Backbeat, 2002)

5   Richards was to contribute also to further Ron Wood solo offerings such as 1975's *Now Look* and 1979's *Gimme Some Neck*.

6   Off-the-cuff examples are Gary Glitter's 'I Didn't Know I Loved You (Till I Saw You Rock 'N' Roll)', 'Rock 'N' Roll Lady' by Showaddywaddy, Wizzard's 'Rock 'N' Roll Winter' and 'Rock 'N' Roll I Gave You The Best Years Of My Life' from Mac Davis (covered in Britain by Kevin Johnson).

7   *Sunday Mirror*, 14 March 2004

8   *The Rolling Stones Chronicle* by M Bonanno (Plexus, 1995)

9   *Keith Richards In HIs Own Words* ed. M St Michael (Omnibus, 1994)

10   *Daily Mail*, 18 July 1990

Chapter 14: The Late Arrival

1   *Keith Richards In His Own Words* ed. M St Michael (Omnibus, 1994)

2   *No Sleep Till Canvey Island: The Great Pub Rock Revolution* by W Birch (Virgin, 2000)

3   Berry's 'No Money Down' would be on the B-side of a 1982 Gibbons single.

4   *Q*, November 1992

5   *New Musical Express*, 10 December 1980

6   *The Rolling Stones Chronicle* by M Bonanno (Plexus, 1995)

7   *Evening Standard*, 14 September 1977

8   *Loose Talk* ed. L Botts (Rolling Stone Press, 1980). Thunders' light-hearted stand on his own addiction was reflected in the title of his solo album, *Too Much Junkie Business*.

9   *The Rolling Stones In Their Own Words* ed. D Dalton and M Farren (Omnibus, 1985)

10   *The Rolling Stones As It Happened: The Classic Interviews* (Chrome Dreams CIS 2002/1, 2001)

11   After emerging from heroin addiction, Clapton began drinking heavily.

12   *The Q/Omnibus Press Rock 'N' Roll Reader* ed. D Kelly (Q/Omnibus, 1994)

Chapter 15: The Community Servant

1 *Keith Richards In His Own Words* ed. M St Michael (Omnibus, 1994)
2 *The Sunday Times*, 2 August 2003
3 'The evil-doer hates the light.'
4 Taken from the transcript of the proceedings.
5 A close friend of Keith Richards for a while, Belushi was to die of a mixed cocaine and heroin overdose on 5 March 1982. One of his final public appearances was at a James Brown show at New York's Studio 54 when, observed Brown, 'John was well out of it that night.' (*James Brown* by J Brown and B Tucker [Fontana, 1988]).
6 On whose forthcoming solo album, 1979's *Troublemaker*, Keith would be heard. He was also to contribute to a later McLagan LP, *Best Of British*.
7 With personnel that included Belinda Carlisle (then calling herself 'Dottie Danger') on drums.
8 *Daily Mail*, 18 July 1990
9 *The Rolling Stones Chronicle* by M. Bonnano (Plexus, 1995)

Chapter 16: The Birthday Boy

1 *The Rolling Stones Chronicle* by M Bonnano (Plexus, 1995)
2 *Woman's Own*, 21 November 1987
3 *Keith Richards In His Own Words* ed. M St Michael (Omnibus, 1994)
4 *New Musical Express*, 2 September 1989
5 *Q*, October 1988
6 *Q*, November 1992
7 *The Rolling Stones As It Happened: The Classic Interviews* (Chrome Dreams CIS 2002/1, 2001)

Chapter 17: The Distant Friend

1 *Q*, August 1990
2 *Jeff Beck: Crazy Fingers* by A Carson (Carson, 1998)
3 *The Rolling Stones Chronicle* by M Bonanno (Plexus, 1995)
4 *Inside Classic Rock Tracks* by R Rooksby (Backbeat, 2001)
5 *Keith Richards In His Own Words* ed. M St Michael (Omnibus, 1994)
6 *Q*, October 1987
7 Johnny Marr, guitarist with The Smiths, whose *Meat Is Murder* had topped the UK album list in 1985, was alleged to have played on a Richards session around this time too.
8 *Daily Mail*, 19 July 1990
9 *Rolling Stone*, 7 September 1989
10 *Sounds*, 16 September 1989

11 *Q*, November 1988

12 *New Musical Express*, 2 September 1989

Chapter 18: The Main Offender

1 *The Sunday Times*, 16 March 2003

2 The Armory was, in 1913, the scene of the International Exhibition of Modern Art, a *succès de scandale* that rippled across the decades.

3 *Kerrang*, 17 December 1992

4 *Keith Richards In His Own Words* ed. M St Michael (Omnibus, 1994)

5 *The Rolling Stones Chronicle* by M Bonanno (Plexus, 1995)

6 *Q*, October 1989

7 *The Rolling Stones As It Happened: The Classic Interviews* (Chrome Dreams CIS 2002/1, 2001)

8 *The Guardian*, 5 September 2003

9 *Sunday Magazine*, 20 August 2003

10 Where Stella McCartney also studied prior to a flourishing career in fashion design.

11 In August 2000, Bert Richards died of a heart attack, aged 85.

12 *The Guardian*, 5 December 2003

13, *New Musical Express*, 1 May 1995)

14 *Q*, September 1990

15 *Best Of Guitar Player*, December 1994

16 *USA Today*, 3 August 1994

17 *St Louis Post-Despatch*, 24 November 1995

18 As well as penning a foreword to Johnson's biography, *Father Of Rock 'N' Roll* by Travis Fitzpatrick (Thomas, Cooke and Co., 1999), Richards also inducted the pianist into the Rock 'N' Roll Hall Of Fame in 2001.

19 *The Sunday Times*, 5 May 1990

20 *The Times*, 13 December 2003

Epilogue: The Greying Eminence

1 *The Sunday Times*, 2 December 2003

2 *The Guardian*, 5 September 2003

Index